Comments on other *Amazing Stories* from readers & reviewers

"*Tightly written volumes filled with lots of wit and humour about famous and infamous Canadians.*"
Eric Shackleton, *The Globe and Mail*

"*The heightened sense of drama and intrigue, combined with a good dose of human interest is what sets* Amazing Stories *apart.*"
Pamela Klaffke, *Calgary Herald*

"*This is popular history as it should be... For this price, buy two and give one to a friend.*"
Terry Cook, a reader from Ottawa, on **Rebel Women**

"*Glasner creates the moment of the explosion itself in graphic detail...she builds detail upon gruesome detail to create a convincingly authentic picture.*"
Peggy McKinnon, *The Sunday Herald,* on **The Halifax Explosion**

"*It was wonderful...I found I could not put it down. I was sorry when it was completed.*"
Dorothy F. from Manitoba on **Marie-Anne Lagimodière**

"*Stories are rich in descri... with a cleve...*"
Mark Weber, *Central Alberta*

"*A compelling read. Bertin...ha... ...iguing tales, which she narrate... ...i of detail.*"
Joyce Glasner, *New Brunswick Reader,* on **Strange Events**

"*The resulting book is one readers will want to share with all the women in their lives.*"
Lynn Martel, *Rocky Mountain Outlook,* on **Women Explorers**

# UNSUNG HEROES OF THE ROYAL CANADIAN NAVY

# UNSUNG HEROES OF THE ROYAL CANADIAN NAVY

## Incredible Tales of Courage and Daring During World War II

**HISTORY**

by Cynthia J. Faryon

PUBLISHED BY ALTITUDE PUBLISHING CANADA LTD.
1500 Railway Avenue, Canmore, Alberta  T1W 1P6
www.altitudepublishing.com
1-800-957-6888

Extreme care has been taken to ensure that all information presented in
this book is accurate and up to date. Neither the author nor the
publisher can be held responsible for any errors.

|  |  |
|---|---|
| Publisher | Stephen Hutchings |
| Associate Publisher | Kara Turner |
| Series Editor | Jill Foran |
| Editor | Dianne Smyth |
| Digital Photo Colouring | Bryan Pezzi |

We acknowledge the financial support of the Government
of Canada through the Book Publishing Industry Development
Program (BPIDP) for our publishing activities.

**Altitude GreenTree Program**
Altitude Publishing will plant twice as many trees as were used
in the manufacturing of this product.

**National Library of Canada Cataloguing in Publication Data**

Faryon, Cynthia J., 1956-
Unsung heroes of the Royal Canadian Navy / Cynthia Faryon.

(Amazing stories)
ISBN 1-55153-765-6

1. Canada. Royal Canadian Navy--History--World War, 1939-1945.
2. Canada. Royal Canadian Navy--Biography. 3. Sailors--Canada--Biography.
4. Heroes--Canada--Biography. I. Title. II. Series: Amazing stories
(Canmore, Alta.)

D779.C2F37 2005      940.54'5971      C2004-906265-4

Printed and bound in Canada by Friesens
2  4  6  8  9  7  5  3

To all the children and grandchildren
of veterans. This is part of your history.

And to Roger, who has stuck by me and supported
me in the writing and research of this book. Without
his belief in me, it would never have been completed.

# Contents

# Prologue

*The great ship stands quietly in the morning sun, anxious to find the waves beneath her hull and thirsty for the company of the saltys who will man her. This great Tribal Class Destroyer was built for war. Adopting the tenacity and stubborn pride of the mateys who took two long years to give her life, she stands proudly in front of the men who will take her into battle.*

*The commissioning ceremony is a brief and simple affair, filled with naval tradition and quiet dignity. At the spoken command the new crew stands at ease in the shadow of the destroyer waiting patiently alongside the dock. All eyes are reverent during the prayer of dedication. The crew stands, heads bowed, arms crossed at the wrists, respectfully holding their caps. And, with a few words from the new captain, they remember their fallen comrades and swear to do this great ship justice in the world's fight for freedom. Downwind, the staccato sounds of shipbuilding remind them that their fight is far from over. For this crew and their ship, it is only the beginning. Not only will this destroyer be their weapon and their protector, it will be their home and their friend.*

*Clustered on the top of old barrels, piles of lumber, and the other vantage points along the dockside, the mateys (the men and women who built her) watch in solemn stillness as*

*the finality of their labours settles on them. They are not offi-
cially part of this ceremony, but with pride and sadness they
watch from a distance. Quietly, they say their goodbyes as the
Canadian naval crew (the saltys), who had arrived just before
the ceremony, lay claim to the mateys' creation.*

*This morning is the end of more than two years of emo-
tional labour for the mateys. From thoughts to blueprints,
from steel to ship, her building had been a grim yet proud
chapter in their lives. Throughout the long months in which
she had grown from an idea to a lethal weapon of war, they
had been touched by the death and destruction that threatened the night skies. The mateys had seen the newsreels of the
bombings in Europe, had witnessed the destruction, and had
welcomed home their dead to their final resting places. They
worked diligently day after day, knowing that many more
Canadian boys would sacrifice their lives before this fight was
finished. If they could have fought they would have, but we
can't all go to war. Some are needed here at home. So, fuelled by
familial stories of loss, the mateys' own incensed spirits entered
the steel they forged as they built their ship, fighting back the
only way they knew how.*

*From where they are gathered they can't hear the words
with which the captain charges the crew. But when the hat
is thrown into the air and the crew cheers, the mateys cheer,
too, with shouts of "Godspeed!" "Make 'em pay!" "Bring her
home safely!"*

*Then reluctantly, and more than a little sadly, the mateys*

## Prologue

*leave their newborn in the hands of the Royal Canadian Navy (RCN). This new "lady" they have created from steel and iron is theirs no longer. She now belongs to the strong young hands of the navy crew who will take her from berth into the vast ocean beyond. They know that as long as there are memories of this great ship and stories shared of her exploits, she, like the lads on board, will never be forgotten. And all the battles, the deaths, the victories, will be remembered with awe and thankfulness for all who served and lived and fought to make this country free.*

# Chapter 1
# The First Canadian Naval Shot of World War II

On September 1, 1939, Adolf Hitler's army and air force cross into Poland. On September 3, Britain declares war on Germany. In a matter of days, most of the world has chosen sides.

After the initial German aggression, there is a pause before the fighting starts. Germany sits quietly waiting and Britain feeds her troops into mainland Europe. The trap is laid and Germany closes in on the Allies. All hell breaks loose with a fury of German fighting machines that leave the British troops breathless and collectively fighting for their lives. As they retreat to the coastline, with their backs against the English Channel, the massacre begins ... then suddenly slows. Like a panther waiting to pounce, the German army keeps the British on the beaches, letting the troops know, with an occasional strafing and a few shells flying overhead, that they can finish the men off at any time.

On a stretch of coast from Dunkirk to the southern port of St. Jean de Luz, two Polish divisions, along with a few French troops, are fighting desperately against the Germans. The situation is frantic and the Allies are being slaughtered like cattle, their young blood soaking the surf-smoothed stones along the beach. What the Brits swore would never happen is happening and thousands of troops are trapped without cover. Mercifully, the air support drops smoke, and the sea mist creeps over the beaches with eerie fingers of cold and damp, providing additional cover. The troops shiver and wait for the final blast that surely must be coming. The Germans, poised for the butchery of those still alive, are left waiting for the final order to finish the job they started.

A desperate cry for help goes out from Britain to Canada for ships to rescue the troops from the beaches of Dunkirk. The invasion of Great Britain is now a definite threat and the war looks all but lost.

And so the miracle that is known as Dunkirk is born. With a mission of mercy in everyone's heart, civilians — in whatever boats they have — brave the Atlantic from the English coast to the beaches of Dunkirk.

With an audacity, courage, and eagerness that humbles the rest of the world, civilians and military alike come to the aid of the troops. Once the boats make it across the Channel, bits and pieces of human tragedy gratefully hoist themselves on board and sail home in anything that will float. They leave behind their artillery, vehicles, ammunition, and many of their fallen. Even a rowboat, one cruelly buffeted by the Atlantic and crudely captained by a young teenager, is considered safer than the beaches and is viewed by the soldiers as godsent.

One of these brave rescuers is Robert "Bob" Timbrell of West Vancouver, British Columbia. British born, he joined the RCN at the outbreak of trouble. Appointed captain of the yacht HMS *Lanthony*, Timbrell makes six successful crossings before disaster hits. Then a German bomb hits the forecastle of the yacht, killing five of his crew members and cutting the fuel line. Limping to shore, the crew and army troops create a jetty out of trucks until the tide lifts the ship back into the water. The fuel line is repaired and Captain Timbrell arms the yacht with spare guns from some of the military vehicles left behind. His foresight serves him well. The boat is attacked by two E-Boats (German Ebling Ships) and he is able to fight them off. In all, Captain Timbrell is responsible for rescuing over 600 troops.

The HMCS *Restigouche* (fondly referred to as "Rustyguts" by her crew), the HMCS *Skeena*, and the HMCS *St. Laurent* ("Sally") are recalled from leave and ordered to ship out to England. A disgruntled lot of sailors begin to straggle back to their ships as dusk settles over the Halifax harbour. And the familiar pipe is heard: "Cable party muster on the forecastle!

... Special sea-duty men close up! ... Hands to stations for leaving harbour!"

The entire group of seamen groan, crawling back to their ships in whatever condition the orders find them, thinking it's simply more convoy duty. The ships make ready and slip their berths, setting a quick course for Plymouth.

Lieutenant Commander Nelson Lay in HMCS *Restigouche* is the senior commander of the group and leads the way across the Atlantic. Lieutenant Commander Henry "Harry" George De Wolf follows in the HMCS *St. Laurent*, and Lieutenant Commander Jimmy Hibbard brings up the rear in the HMCS *Skeena*. Commander Wallace Creery is captain of the HMCS *Fraser*, already in service overseas. They are all Canadian seamen and Canadian ships.

Nelson Lay, wanting to impress the British with Canadian seamanship, orders drills for the ships during the crossing. Lay slows the vessels from 16 knots, increases speed, pulls ahead, and then orders a reverse course. These exercises are conducted after dark, with all the ships blacked out and running on visuals only, because none of the ships have radar. The progress across the Atlantic is slow and the men complain to each other about how long the crossing is taking. After all, they now have a mission. Their troops are trapped and dying on a foreign beach and all of them want to come to the rescue, like the cavalry in an American western.

Harry De Wolf is also impatient. "You know," he grumbles to the bridge crew, "Lay and I will be known in the RN

(Royal Navy) as 'those two Canadians, De Wolf and De Lay.'"
But upon their arrival in Plymouth the first lord of the admiralty seems not to notice their "de lay," and he sends them a message of welcome: "The presence of the units of the Royal Canadian Navy in our midst inspires us to a still harder effort. Confident both of your skill and of your valour we wish you good luck in the fierce and exacting toil which lies before you."

However, it turns out the Canadians have missed the main evacuation and are ordered for clean-up along the continental coast.

The *Restigouche* patrols off the coastal town of Le Havre, and then heads for St. Valery to pick up the 51st Highlanders. There are pockets of Allied troops still left onshore, destroying all oil and machinery before retreating off the beaches. The flames mount so high in the sky that they can be seen at sea, and a dark grey pall hangs heavily along the coastline, filling the sinuses with an acrid smoke.

Arriving at St. Valery at about 5:30 a.m., Rustyguts finds another destroyer, a liner, half-a-dozen transports, several railway ferries, and many small boats evacuating the French and British wounded. Confusion reigns, and the Highlanders are nowhere to be found. Lieutenant Commander Lay takes command of the situation and tells his first lieutenant, Debby Piers, to send someone ashore to contact General Fortune of the Highlanders. The ships are sitting ducks this close to shore batteries, and no one knows exactly where and when the Germans will wake up and attack. Piers decides to volunteer himself. He came to fight in the war, and he feels that a little adventure ashore would suit him.

St. Valery, off the coast of France, is a village with a population of about 1000. It has a stone pier where the river joins the sea, and sheer cliffs separate the shore from the village. The Canadian ships keep a vigilant eye on those cliffs while they await word on the Highlanders, as there is no way of knowing what's advancing on the other side. A small cutter is launched for Piers and he climbs aboard, not knowing what he will find onshore. He's given a time limit, with orders to signal back as soon as he has word.

The small boat bounces through the surf toward the chaos onshore, and Piers is sure the whine of the engine will bring the Germans running. Heading full-speed at the beach, he hits a rock and bends the propeller, but everything else stays intact. Dragging the boat up onshore, he ties it off on an encroaching branch while glancing nervously around him. The beach is littered with shrapnel, torn uniforms, blast holes from shelling, and dried blood. A body rocks back and forth in the surf, entrails fanning out behind it like the tentacles of a jellyfish. Seagulls are wheeling overhead, and here and there a few of the birds fight over remains that Piers really doesn't want to identify. He steps over a lone boot and tries not to think of what might have happened to the man who was wearing it. Medics are still clearing the dead and the dying, so Piers leaves them to their macabre tasks and hikes up a trail to the cliff top.

Armed merchant cruiser HMCS *Prince Robert* during a 1943 refit that
made her Canada's first auxiliary anti-aircraft cruiser

Following the sound of machine-gun fire, Piers finds
General Fortune of the 51st Highlanders aways inland. He
tries to explain to the general that the ships have been
ordered to take his men off the coast. The general has been
out of touch with his headquarters for several days. And
since the French commander in the area hasn't yet ordered
his troops to evacuate, the general decides not to go either.
He doesn't like the navy coming to "rescue" him, nor does he
like the idea that his men will leave before the French troops.
General Fortune decides that if he continues to hold the
perimeter of the Dunkirk evacuation, more soldiers will get
safely off to fight another day. Neither he nor Lay have been

told that the main evacuation is finished, or that the remaining troops are surrounded by the German panzer divisions led by General Rommel.

In the distance the pounding boom of the enemy guns hits the eardrums with a dull thud. Piers can feel his blood pressure rise as he looks nervously around him, expecting the Germans to appear at any moment. "But we've got five, six, seven ships here, sir," he argues with the general. "We can take off thousands, and Captain Lay has received orders ..." But nothing Piers says persuades the general to abandon the fight. Piers is told to get back to his ship.

The machine-gun fire increases and shells start whizzing overhead. On the other side of the hill the sound of German tanks fills the air and men are running for cover. The French troops on the beaches decide not to wait for the order to evacuate, and gratefully accept transport on the waiting Canadian ships. Piers narrowly escapes the area as all hell breaks loose. Behind him, the 51st are captured and spend the next four years in German Prisoner of War (POW) camps.

Once back in his cutter, Piers discovers to his dismay that the boat will only make half-a-knot due to the damaged propeller. He signals the *Restigouche*, which is lying about four kilometres offshore and waiting anxiously for his news. By this time, the ship has been joined by the *St. Laurent*, which is filled with French troops. Lay gives orders to proceed closer inshore and to go and get Piers, rather than wait for him to reach them. The German guns are getting closer and the top of the cliffs are filled with tank movement.

The *Restigouche* reaches Piers's little boat, hooks it up to pulleys, and starts hoisting it up the side of the destroyer. Suddenly, panzer tanks open fire. Shells whiz overhead, pinging on the metal hull, splashing in the waves, exploding loudly. The crew scrambles, some to man the guns and give the Germans what for, and others to load the ammunition. Meanwhile, others struggle to hoist the cutter safely on deck. Smoke from the guns mixes with the burning of vehicles, and the noise drives the men's adrenaline higher. Whistle ... whoosh ... splat ... Kaboom! And a splatter of sea water hits the deck. Whistle ... whoosh ... splat ... Kaboom! And everyone ducks. Well, almost everyone. Lay is sitting calmly while his men are scrambling, and De Wolf, on the *St. Laurent*, wants in on the action.

Under a full head of steam, the *St. Laurent* comes to the rescue. De Wolf, often referred to as "hard-over Harry," isn't known to smile a great deal. But when he opens up with his 4.7-inch guns aimed at the cliffs above St. Valery, he has a huge grin on his face. His is the first Canadian ship to fire on the enemy in World War II. The crew cheers. They had come to fight the Germans, and finally the action has begun. With every boom of the gun the ship lurches and shudders. Pungent smoke fills the air and the men continue to cheer. "Hard-over-Harry" is still smiling broadly.

The *Restigouche*, after regrouping, joins in the foray. Both Canadian destroyers bang away at the tanks on top of the cliffs. The orders are shouted above the din, ammunition flies, hoisted from below decks and into the hands of the gun crew. Load! Load! LOAD! ... Wham! The *Restigouche* shudders and below decks the crew hears the strain on the hull and feels the recoil. Then the German guns answer back. Boom! ... Kathunk! Shells fly over the ships about a metre above the bridge. Whoooosh! They splash into the water, sending up an impressive spout. With the sound of each shell bursting, everyone on deck flings his body flat and holds his breath — even though once the shell explodes the danger is past. Commander Lay watches the action, still sitting calmly on his chair on the bridge.

The German guns straddle Rustyguts, trying to get a fix on their target. Boom! Whoosh! Too far on the port side. Boom! Whoosh! Too much to starboard. They're short again and again, trying to pinpoint the target. Commander Lay orders the guns to continue firing at the tanks while the ship zigzags, making things more difficult for the Germans. Shell splinters cut through the rigging and ping! ping! ping! off the upper and lower decks, leaving a ringing in the ears. Bullets ricochet, and the harsh smell from the guns fills everyone's nostrils. Those below decks hear the booms, feel the ship react, and keep the ammo coming. Dishes smash in the wild manoeuvres. Sailors grab whatever is screwed down in order to stay on their feet. The tension on board is mounting. This is no escort duty. This is war.

As soon as Piers is back on deck, he makes his way to

the bridge to report to the captain. By this time Rustyguts is doing 32 knots and zigzagging to avoid the shelling. The officer of the watch, the yeoman of signals, and the rest of the crew on the bridge are ducking down behind the canvas wind dodgers, supposedly to avoid the shells. The captain watches them and chuckles, as the canvas couldn't possibly offer protection against a 3-inch shell. With a slight smile still on his face, he looks at Piers amidst the smoke and noise. "Well, Number One?" Lay asks him. A shell explodes off the port side and Piers ducks. The captain barely flinches. Piers makes his report, ducking when shrapnel whizzes overhead or the guns boom. Yet there is Captain Lay, with his steel helmet on, sitting calmly in his chair as if nothing is happening.

After the report, since there are no more troops to evacuate, Lay orders the *St. Laurent* up the coast to continue to engage shore batteries while Rustyguts makes for Plymouth at 32 knots.

When the *Restigouche* nears the English harbour, a fighter plane dives at the ship from out of the sun. Lay sits straight up in his chair and yells, "Open fire!" He shows more excitement and emotion at this moment than during the whole battle off the coast. But the crew is taken by surprise and none of the 4.7-inch guns can be loaded and fired. After the aircraft has flown past, a few pitiful rounds from a Lewis gun splatter the sky aimlessly. The fighter circles and flashes a message to the vessel by Aldus light, "Damn poor shooting. But at least you're awake." The plane is British, piloted by a

Canadian fly boy with time on his hands who thought the navy boys looked bored. "I hope he has plenty to do in the battle later," is Lay's curt response.

Lay sets course to join the HMS *Calcutta* and the HMCS *Fraser*. They have just gone up the Gironde River, near Bordeaux, France, to blow up everything the advancing Germans might make use of. The HMCS *Restigouche* is to rendezvous with them, and escort them back to Plymouth.

But this never comes to pass.

# Chapter 2
# HMCS *Fraser* — Collision at Sea

I t's the evening of June 25, 1940. The Canadian ships HMCS *Restigouche* and HMCS *Fraser*, as well as the British ship HMS *Calcutta*, are on a return trip from the coast of France. The ships are without radar, the night is dark, and the convoy is blacked out. In the quiet of the night, the whoosh and slap of the ocean on the hull of the destroyers is strangely peaceful. Too peaceful, think some of the crew. Dunkirk is fresh on their minds and every one of them is thinking about what the Nazis will do next.

The *Fraser* drops back to take a visual bearing of those behind, and the crew is suddenly ordered to change stations at top speed. The ship is preparing to make its way from the Gironde River estuary and across the Channel to England.

The Royal Navy's *Calcutta* is a 4290-tonne light cruiser, built at the end of World War I. On this occasion, Vice Admiral A.T.B. Curteis, flag officer commanding, Second Cruiser Squadron, is on board and in command of this small group. With tensions running high on the ships, most of the crews are starved for sleep.

The admiral orders a reduced speed of 20 knots and alters course, putting the *Fraser* on the *Calcutta's* starboard bow and the *Restigouche* on the cruiser's port quarter. Then he orders the destroyers to form a single line, reducing the speed of the formation to 14 knots. The *Calcutta* is to take the lead, with the *Fraser* next, and the *Restigouche* in the rear. At least, that is the plan. Lieutenant Commander Lay, captain of the *Restigouche*, temporarily increases speed to close up the formation behind the cruiser and then alters to starboard, being careful to leave the *Fraser* room to pull into the middle. Like synchronized swimmers, the *Restigouche* speeds forward while the *Fraser* swings inward to turn down *Calcutta's* starboard side — or so the *Calcutta* expects. But the *Fraser* is zigzagging without any intention of falling in line — the ship never received the order.

The commanding officer of the *Fraser*, Wallace Creery, tells the officer of the watch, Lieutenant Harold Groos, to carry on with the manoeuvres as scheduled. Groos gives the order "Port 10!" Creery tells Groos to increase speed and "swing a hard over!"

The *Calcutta* sees the move and misinterprets the

intention, expecting the *Fraser* to pass in front of the *Calcutta*. However, the *Fraser* is turning inward, to pass down the *Calcutta*'s port side and make a complete turn in order to finish off the zigzag. Curteis, concerned about how close the *Fraser* will pass on the Calcutta's port side, orders "Starboard wheel!" and gives one short blast, cutting off the *Fraser*'s complete turn. When the *Calcutta* sees the *Fraser* turn sharply to port, the commander realizes the ships are on a collision course and orders the engines to full reverse.

Seeing the *Calcutta*'s change in direction and speed, Commander Creery realizes the *Fraser* can't turn sharply enough to avoid a collision. Creery takes over the wheel, ordering "Port 20!" and then "Hard-a-port!" The *Fraser* groans, dishes go flying, rivets pop, and those shipmates who are asleep in bunks roll onto the floor.

Creery realizes too late that he can't get the ship clear by a port turn. He then orders "Hard to starboard!" trying to pass across the bow of the larger ship, gunning the engines to outrun it and lessen the impact. The *Calcutta*'s bow surges forward. Those on the bridge watch in mortal fascination as the bow of the *Calcutta* slices into their ship. The *Fraser* rips in two behind the "B" gun. The metal peels back from the hull and sparks fly in the night sky, filling the darkness with the shrill screech of ripping metal, mixing with the screams of the injured. The forward part of the ship breaks off, bobbing a few metres away like an apple in a tub of water. The wheel-house and bridge structure are scooped onto the *Calcutta*'s forecastle by the ship's forward thrust, ending up in one piece on the cruiser's bow. Creery leads the few bridge personnel to safety by jumping to the forecastle deck of the *Calcutta*. Able Seaman Todeus of the *Fraser* is yelling for help, as his feet have been badly crushed in the collision. Creery returns to the wrecked wheelhouse and rescues Todeus and Russ Milray, who was also badly crushed when the *Calcutta* was hit. Russ doesn't look good, and is taken to the sick bay for immediate medical attention.

The *Calcutta* lowers a small boat for the *Fraser*'s survivors and surges on, signalling to Lieutenant Commander Lay in the *Restigouche* to pick up any remaining crew. Those left stranded watch the cruiser disappear into the darkness.

Tom Kellington is a stoker on watch in the engine room of the *Fraser* at the time of the ramming. The engines are still going astern, there is a hesitation, and then the lights go out. He doesn't feel much of a shock, no bumps or grinding noise can be heard above the throbbing of the engines. The lights simply die. Then the engines die. And then, complete silence.

Chief Engine Room Artificer Kent sends Kellington up the hatch to see what has happened. Kellington sees what he thinks is a rammed submarine tilted upwards, not realizing it's the *Fraser*'s forward end. The forward boiler room is flooding, and when the tank suctions give way, everything dies.

Not sensing the seriousness of the situation, Kellington picks up some of his jerseys, which have fallen from the drying line around the air pump. When he gets back to the engine room it's empty. He drops the jerseys and gets out fast. Kellington jumps over the side of the wounded ship and is hauled into the *Fraser's* whaler. "Give me an oar!" he roars, and sets to work, ready to row to England if necessary.

Commander Lay, in the *Restigouche*, has not been told that the *Fraser* has been rammed. He is only told to pick up survivors. Seeing the damage, Lay isn't sure if the ship was torpedoed or if it hit a submerged rock. He is amazed to find that the after-part of the Canadian ship is floating perfectly well. But there is no bow and no bridge, only the ship's smokestacks and stern.

It is now after 10 p.m. The easiest way to rescue the survivors still on board is to pull alongside the wreck at the back end of the ship and hold her fast. Scramble nets are tossed over the side for the survivors to climb to safety. "Heave up, lads," the men are encouraged. "Pass up the injured first, men."

Meanwhile, the severed bow drifts away in the darkness, upside down, trapping some of the crew below the waterline. Muffled banging fills the night air, and those already rescued watch anxiously to see what will happen to their trapped crew mates. Lay lowers his whaler, giving command of the rescue vessel to Canadian Lieutenant David Walter. Also ordered aboard are Lieutenant Harold Groos and Leading Signalman P.E. Palmer who has a hand-held night light for flashing communications. Groos motors slowly in the dark swells and drifts of the icy waters, pulling exhausted men from the chilly depths. The whaler fills up, and he orders the engines killed to better hear the men still in the water. When the whaler pulls back to the *Restigouche,* the *Fraser's* propellers on the floating wreck begin turning. The *Fraser* rolls down on the whaler, throwing everyone into the water. One of the rescuers is tossed into the water and sinks. No one can reach him in time. Everyone else manages to reach the nets and safely climb on board. Those who are left on the *Fraser* start passing medical supplies and bottles of liquor up to their doctor, Blair McLean, who is now aboard the *Restigouche* and caring for the injured. Most of the men have fuel oil in their eyes and wounds. It floats on the water, and here and there small pools have ignited, giving off an eerie light over the swells.

The *Fraser's* bow then capsizes, throwing more men into the icy seas. Carley floats (life rafts with slatted bottoms) are tossed out to them. The desperate calls from injured shipmates lost in the waves will haunt the survivors for the rest of their lives. The seamen feverishly work to save all who remain alive.

Finally, all who can be saved are safely aboard *Restigouche.* There is suddenly a loud sucking noise. The other half of the *Fraser,* floating high in the water and wallowing keel up, loses both forward guns as they fall into the water. The bow briefly rights again. Those trapped below tumble out and rush to the side nearest the *Restigouche.* They stretch out their arms and call out, hoping for rescue. With a whoosh! the *Fraser* turns keel up again, flinging the men into the water. Boats, Carley floats, and life buoys are lowered.

Men are yelling. The waves relentlessly grab and pull the men down. More survivors are brought on board.

The *Restigouche* is filled with people. Along with 59 evacuees from St. Jean de Luz, there are 11 officers and 96 men from the fore part of the *Fraser*. The wounded lie everywhere, with burns, cuts, and fuel-filled eyes, as well as broken bones and serious injuries caused by crushing. Kellington works frantically with Dr. McLean. Kellington is rushing back and forth to the engine room to heat water under the air pump because there are no hot water taps. He then runs the water to the doctor, who uses it to wash the oil off the injured. Before scrubbing the wounds, the doctor gives each man a tot of rum to help with the pain.

In the early morning mist, the harbour of Plymouth, England, lies sleepy and quiet. The throbbing of engines is heard, and through the fog a ghostly apparition creeps slowly to port. The *Calcutta*'s bow nudges the docking bay, and, gruesomely positioned on her forecastle deck, is the bridge of the *Fraser*.

Russ Milray, one of the men who was badly crushed, spent nearly two years in hospital in Devonport recovering from his injuries. He had more breaks in his body than could be counted. Gangrene set in quickly, and it seemed at first that Russ was a hopeless case. His legs had to be amputated to cut out all the infection, but gangrene set in again in the stumps. He had surgery after surgery to cut away the dead and dying flesh, and to save as much as could be saved. Still he hung in there, with that quiet stubbornness Canadians are famous for. Years later, in 1947, one of his Navy buddies from the *Fraser* met Russ Milray and his wife at a theatre in Toronto. Russ was smiling, cracking jokes, and looking healthy.

As for the *Fraser*, although the ship was done for, the adventures of its survivors were far from over. A few months later ...

# Chapter 3
# "Déjà vu, Margaree"

hen HMCS *Fraser* is lost in June 1940, arrangements are immediately made by the Canadian government to purchase a replacement from the Royal Navy. The HMS *Diana* has served in the Mediterranean and the Home Fleets, and the higher-ups decide she is the perfect replacement for the *Fraser*. She is sent to Albert Docks in London to be refitted, and is then commissioned as HMCS *Margaree*.

During the ship's refit the Germans hit the harbour with a vengeance. Twelve ships are damaged during one night's raid. But the *Margaree* is not touched. During the next night of bombing, a couple of sticks of explosives straddle her, and one sinks under the ship without exploding. The next morning the dockyard mateys brave the threat and pull her along the jetty

*"Déjà vu,* Margaree"

a few hundred metres to get clear of the explosives. As soon as she is at a safe distance the bombs explode, sending a plume of water high into the air. The *Margaree* remains intact.

Word that HMCS *Margaree* is a "lucky" ship spreads among her new crew. This is comforting news since the majority of the crew are survivors from the HMCS *Fraser.* Thirteen of the wounded have recovered sufficiently to be assigned to the *Margaree.* Yes, they are all happy to hear she is a lucky ship.

Two of those reassigned to the *Margaree* are Dr. McLean and Lieutenant Landymore. Landymore was married a couple of months after surviving the ramming of the *Fraser,* and two months later here he is, climbing the gangplank of the *Fraser's* replacement. As he steps foot on deck, he pats his front shirt pocket, where he keeps a picture of his wife, and hopes that the rumours are true. Landymore is determined to return to port safely to rejoin his bride.

The *Margaree* and her crew sail to Londonderry on a shakedown and workup cruise. One of the two sub-lieutenants has to sleep in the forward cabin, directly under the bridge. It's a tiny space with low head clearance. The occupant is chosen by the flip of a coin, something that will be talked about for years to come. Sub-Lieutenant Bob Timbrell wins the toss and makes himself comfortable in the cabin near the wardroom. It's a bigger cabin with a higher ceiling.

After Londonderry, the HMCS *Margaree* is ordered on convoy duty. The convoy gathers and sails on October 20,

35

1940. The ships travel in four columns, with the merchant vessel *Port Fairy* leading the port column, followed by the SS *Jamaica Planter*. The other three ships are in single columns starboard at 400-metre intervals. The group is travelling quicker than normal, and in a straight line instead of the evasive zigzagging most escorts use to avoid being an easy target for German U-boats. The *Margaree's* crew is uneasy during the entire voyage. Even though she is rumoured to be a lucky boat, too many things don't feel right. She is like a cat that has survived nine times, and they are all wondering what will happen the next time her life is threatened.

The second night out the weather worsens. Rain squalls splatter the bridge screens, lessening visibility. All voyages are conducted under blackout conditions, and even with a scant 400 metres between ships, the crews experience the feeling of isolation. The wind begins to kick up the swells, snatching the tops off the waves and tearing at the rigging on deck. The salt in the wind stings the faces of those on watch and blinds their eyes, making the upper deck almost impassable. The ships in each column climb the swells to the top of each crest, rain splatters the bridges and upper decks in torrential blasts, and the lookouts take their visual bearings. Then the ships plunge back down into the watery valley with sea water swooshing over the sides of the vessels, over the forward gun, then crashing against the superstructure, which jars the hull and strains the rivets.

Life below deck is a tangle of wet uniforms and fitful

sleeps. Everything is damp, clothes smell of wet wool, body odour, and fish. Most men sleep with their life belts and clothing on. Cooking is impossible with the rolling of the vessels, so meals consist of sandwiches eaten to the constant and violent bruising motion of the ocean. Drinking a cup of coffee or kye (very strong, thick hot chocolate) becomes a balancing act, with the drinker wearing more than he sw–allows. Even using the head (the toilet on a ship) is a life-endangering event. Sitting on the throne is more than risky as the boat jostles and pitches, but flushing is even worse. If one does this at the wrong time, one chances being douched to death as the sea overpowers the valves and plumbing, soaking the sitter with whatever is in the bowl and pipes, and, even worse, creating a vacuum that threatens the continuation of the family name.

The *Margaree* is approximately two to three kilometres ahead of the convoy. She drops back closer to the group because of poor visibility. The signalman lets the rest of the convoy know of the change in speed. But in these conditions it's anyone's guess whether or not someone has seen the flashes. At midnight the first lieutenant turns the watch over to the relief, and advises him that the ship is gradually allowing the convoy to catch up with her.

The gun's crew is told to leave only two men at the gun mountings so the others can find some relief from the squall. Water is constantly drenching everything in fits from the sea and from the downpour from the sky. The men are miserable.

Taking pity on them, the officers tell them they can spell each other off, two at a time, giving leave to the others to find whatever comfort is available.

Aboard the *Port Fairy*, the first indication of trouble is in the early morning of October 22 at about one o'clock, when her chief officer observes the *Margaree* off the starboard bow. She is crossing too close in front for the *Port Fairy*'s speed and the roughness of the sea. He stops his engines, and when he sees that the *Margaree* is surging to port on the cresting waves, he orders full reverse, putting his wheel hard-a-port and sounding three short blasts to warn the destroyer as well as the *Jamaica Planter* behind him. He can't move to starboard because of the other convoy ships, and the *Margaree* — oblivious to the danger closing in on her — is continuing on her original path.

The *Port Fairy*'s engines hesitate in the tossing seas. Full reverse isn't engaging due to the swells lifting and surging forward in the current. The *Margaree*'s lookouts, struggling to see in the rain and wind, don't realize the other vessel is so close. They alter to port to take a wave, and cut directly across the bow of the *Port Fairy*. The timing could not possibly be worse for the two ships. The *Port Fairy* surges ahead on the force of a swell, and the *Margaree* hesitates in an undertow. The bridge crew in the *Port Fairy* give a yell and hang on tight, blasting the ship's horn to warn the crews of both ships, yet helpless to stop the collision. The *Margaree*'s bridge crew look up in time to see the bow of the *Port Fairy* descending on them from above. The men yell and brace themselves. Only God knows if they will survive the crash.

The *Port Fairy's* stem slices through the *Margaree's* bridge area, breaking the ship in half. The screams of the bridge crew are snatched away by the relentless wind and waves. Those below, still sleeping in their hammocks, haven't a chance. They receive no warning. The sub-lieutenant who lost the coin toss for sleeping quarters is asleep in his bunk below the bridge when the *Port Fairy* slices through his cabin. He is never seen again. The howl of the Atlantic squall is punctuated by the throbbing of the turbines. It drowns out the scraping of metal on metal and the ripping of the hull. The men crushed or broken are instantly thrown overboard, or pinned where they stand watch. Those alive know that when the ship begins to sink, they will go with her. Their home, their ship, will forever be their coffin.

The whole bow section of the *Margaree* sinks immediately. The "B" gun crew, who were ordered off the watch, miraculously survive the crash. The captain of the gun, who ordered the others to get out of the weather a short time before the collision, is at his post and watches in fascinated horror as the bow of the *Port Fairy* drives over him and the guns.

First Lieutenant Pat Russell is the senior surviving officer in the stern section. Without a bow, it's obvious the forward bulkheads will soon buckle. He orders everyone left to abandon ship.

Bob Timbrell had come off watch an hour earlier and was, at the time of the collision, asleep in his cabin beneath the after torpedo tubes. The impact broke the fuel tanks and his cabin is now drenched in fuel. He is thrown out of his bunk, landing hard, and tossed like green salad in the oil-fuel.

As there is nothing he can do about getting the stinking stuff off him, he grabs his greatcoat to protect himself from the weather up top, and rushes to the ladder. The electrical switchboard operator (Able Bodied Seaman Holman) and the ship's doctor (Blair McLean) are already at the ladder struggling to open the hatch to the upper deck. There are no engine noises now — only the sea pounding at the broken hull, and the creaking and groaning of a ship in the throes of death.

"She's sinking," says the doctor in a daze, reliving the collision of the HMCS *Fraser*. The sea had claimed the *Fraser*, and it seems to those who had survived the first collision that fate has come to claim them. The HMCS *Margaree* is no longer a lucky ship.

Bob Timbrell helps the others with the hatch, but their combined pushing and banging won't budge it. They search for something to batter it with. There is nothing. The three men can hear the sea boiling around the vessel. What's left of the ship groans, as if in pain. Trying not to panic, they decide that one of them will have to be used as a battering ram. As the lightest and the longest, Bob is lifted up by the doctor and the electrician to be used as leverage against the unwilling hatch.

## "*Déjà vu,* Margaree"

"Stiffen those legs Timbrell!" they order him. With stiffened legs, poor Bob is hammered against the hatch feet-first. After a couple of tries, the hatch bursts open and the two fall on the deck, dropping Bob back down the ladder. He lands hard, breaking three or four ribs. The ramming party scuttles out. The "ram" picks himself up and follows the other two through the hatch and onto the deck, which is slick with fuel and sea water. Fire has broken out, and Timbrell realizes with a sick feeling in his stomach that, doused in oil as he is, his potential for becoming a human torch is very real.

Another surviving officer is Landymore. He and Russell climb forward to see if any men are trapped. The ship is as silent as a tomb. There are no shouts, not even the sound of escaping steam. There is simply the slapping of the sea, the wallowing of the wreck, and the empty sound of missing men. Landymore swallows hard and pulls his wife's picture from out of his front pocket. Wiping the splatter of rain off it, he takes a deep breath and exhales slowly. He will survive. He has to.

Russell and Landymore continue to comb the wreckage until they find the ramming party on deck. In the dark they can all see the *Port Fairy* alongside, struggling to stay close to the *Margaree* in the tossing seas. The group stare in silence at the hole where the forward end of their beloved ship is supposed to be. The forward end of their ship, and their crew mates, are gone.

Stunned, and with a weird feeling hitting the pit of their

stomachs, they are frozen in indecision. The surreal circumstances of their situation have them momentarily at a loss. Here they are, standing on a deck without a bridge or a forecastle, just the funnels and after end. There are supposed to be crew members in the engine room, the boiler room. There are supposed to be depth-charge crews and those sleeping aft. But the small group is standing alone, gaping in horror.

Both ships stop and the eerie silencing of the naval engines is filled with the violence of the squall. Buffeted by the wind, the hull of the wreck grinds and screeches on that of the rescue ship in teeth-clenching steel on steel. To McLean and Landymore, it's an all too familiar scene. A few scant months ago, they had heard the same sounds on the *Fraser*. Is it too soon to hope they are survivors of this collision, too? "Déjà vu, *Margaree*," whispers Landymore.

McLean and Timbrell leave the group to look for any men killed, injured, or trapped below. But there are no injuries left on board this time. To McLean's astonishment, the members of the crew either died or escaped injury completely. All men left living have found their way on deck. There is no one left alive below.

The disbelief is short-lived. There is work to be done. There are 10 depth charges set to 50 feet on the wreck, and these have to be made safe before they explode and destroy what's left of the *Margaree*, including the men onboard and on the *Port Fairy*. A couple of these charges have broken free and are careening dangerously to and fro across the deck with every swell. Russell orders Timbrell and Holman to deal with them, and the men scramble to get them under control. The four men breathe a sigh of relief when the explosives are finally set on "safe."

The *Port Fairy*, lying alongside the damaged destroyer, is crashing up and down against the wreck with each swell. Ladders are thrown down the sides for the survivors, and 28 seamen leap off the lunging wreck, clinging desperately to the side of the freighter for a breath, and then scrambling up and over to safety. A wave hits. Two men half jump and are half thrown as they leap off the pitching broken vessel. They lose their grip on the oily ladders and fall into the churning water between the ships. The *Port Fairy* plunges to the bottom of the swell, the wreck rises to the crest, and the two hulls smash together with a sickening, grinding thud. There are muffled cries as the two men are crushed between the hulls, their broken bodies sinking beneath the sea. The last that Lieutenant Landymore sees of his fellow shipmates is their hands reaching out of the waves before slowly disappearing.

The ships drift apart and four men are left on board the *Margaree*: Russell, Landymore, Timbrell, and Holman. The *Port Fairy* backs clear to avoid damage as the squall is worsening and they've been without the engines for long enough. The remaining *Margaree* men are on their own. A small Carley float captures their attention and Timbrell and Holman climb on top of the torpedo tubes to wrestle it from where it's stored. Grabbing either side of the float, they haul it on deck.

It is by now about 2:30 a.m., cold and dark, the squall all but blown out. The *Port Fairy* is out of sight and the remaining men are alone with the hollow wreck. The convoy has also moved on, adding to their sense of abandonment. There is a fresh breeze blowing. They are 800 kilometres west of Ireland. It's a long way to swim or paddle but they have incentive — on the one hand, the ocean is cold and wet, on the other, the wreck is sinking.

Timbrell passes the raft's line to Landymore as they prepare to throw the Carley float overboard. He wraps the cord once around his wrist and grasps the end, planting his feet firmly on deck so the float won't drift away when it hits the water. Timbrell and Holman heave the heavy raft over the side, their adrenaline pumping and hearts pounding. The raft sails high into the air and a long way from the *Margaree*. Too late they realize the line is only four feet long and Landymore is a small thin man. The line snaps taught and Landymore gives a yell as he sails over the side with the raft. The other three watch in horror as he hits the water with a splat and disappears from sight. The water is covered with fuel and when Landymore resurfaces, still holding on to the rope, he's spluttering and choking from the salt water he's inhaled. He looks up at the three men on deck as they look down at him. Then he holds up the rope, still firmly grasped in his hand. His face is glowing with oil from the wreck, the water is frigid, and he's still choking, but he has a great big smile on his face. "Landymore, did I give you permission to leave the ship?" Russell asks.

## "*Déjà vu*, Margaree"

The remaining three jump into the ocean and pull themselves into the raft. They manage to paddle to safety and the *Port Fairy* returns an hour later and picks them up.

One hundred and forty-one men died that October night of 1940. Eighty-six of the 141 who went down with the *Margaree* had survived the *Fraser*'s collision, only to die on her replacement.

# *Chapter 4*
# May I Have Your Autograph?

The first settlers in northern Saskatchewan looked at the vastness of the prairies and renamed the desolate landscape Prince Albert, since most of them couldn't pronounce the Native name *Waskesiu*. A hundred years later, the HMCS *Waskesiu* stands forlornly at the dock in Halifax, waiting to be boarded by her crew. And like the early Saskatchewan settlers, the *Waskesiu* will battle the elements, against all odds, to achieve her goal. There are great hopes resting on this Canadian-built frigate, and promises that this new breed of anti-submarine escort ship will be more effective against the enemy than the corvettes.

The HMCS *Waskesiu*, under Lieutenant Commander James Fraser, and the HMS *Nene*, under Commander J.D.

Birch, join the SC-153 (slow convoy) as they move toward the United Kingdom east of mid-ocean. The convoy includes tankers with much-needed fuel. It is literally surrounded by escorts: 5 destroyers, 4 frigates, 11 captain's class frigates, 4 corvettes, 2 anti-submarine trawlers, and 1 rescue tug.

A convoy is like a small city at sea. There's the lead ship, which is the head of government, there is a town doctor, there are fuel ships and supply ships. The little frigates and corvettes are like policemen walking the beat. They keep the laggers moving and keep order in the ranks. Onshore, life holds many unexpected events, and similar events happen at sea. Someone gets sick and the doctor is needed. The challenge in the middle of the ocean is how to get the doctor to the patient. Sometimes it's by motor launch. Other times it's by ship transfer with a pulley system, the doctor sliding down the cable to the deck of the other vessel.

At all times, Plymouth Headquarters tracks the U-boat activity in the Atlantic, and signals each convoy with the day's enemy activities. On the other side, each U-boat reports their position to their own headquarters in Germany. Like a complicated ballet, the Allied ships adjust course to avoid the U-boats, and the U-boats adjust their course to intercept. If the Allies are lucky, the convoys outmanoeuvre and outrun the U-boats.

SC-153 crawls steadily eastward, and it doesn't take long for the commander of this convoy to see that they won't be able to escape the Germans. All they can do is remain alert

Canadian crew men aboard the HMCS *Waskesiu*

and hope that the weather is bad enough to keep the U-boats under the surface.

On February 23 the day breaks dark and gloomy. The German submarine *U-257* is heading home after missing a rendezvous with a German blockade-runner. She is unaware of the convoy in her path. At 11 p.m. the U-boat discovers the group of Allied ships, and sets her sites on the HMCS *Waskesiu*. Commander Heinz Rahe orders the U-boat to dive, choosing to avoid confrontation because the submarine is short of supplies.

Early the next morning, a few minutes after two o'clock, *Waskesiu* Petty Officer M.J.T. Fortune, who is the asdic's (sonar radar's) first operator, discovers the U-boat on his asdic. The asdic's range is two kilometres, weather permitting. The *Waskesiu* has a very narrow margin for striking the U-boat, as the German sub can dive, zigzag, kill all engines and sink, or change to full speed ahead to avoid confrontation.

Manitoban Walter A. Fogg, the ship's telegraphist, holds his breath. The crew are excited to be in on the action. The captain of the *Waskesiu* slows the speed. Ping ... all that can be heard is breathing ...

"Hush, everyone," someone whispers.

"Shhhhhh ..." is the answering chorus.

Ping ... Ping ... Beep!

"There she is."

Ping ... Beep! Ping ... Beep!

"She's moving left, captain."

Canadian Lieutenant Commander Fraser has been in command of the *Waskesiu* for only 19 days. He slows the speed and orders a hedgehog attack first (unlike depth charges, hedgehogs need to strike the target in order to detonate). "Load! Load! LOAD!" the command is shouted down the line. Whumph! ... and the small frigate recoils with the power of the release. "Full speed ahead!" the captain yells, and the small boat leaps on top of the waves to avoid being caught by the explosions.

The ocean erupts and the sub is jarred but unharmed.

Rahe, the German commander, orders the U-boat deeper. He closes his eyes for a millisecond, trying to guess the thoughts of the man in charge of the ship on the surface. Fraser does the same. And as each crawls into the mind of the enemy, the two crews wait for the next order.

A flare is launched to mark the spot for the next attack. Fraser orders a speed of 15 knots, hard-a-port, and then back. The *Waskesiu* jumps and groans with the release of another charge then races away from the site once more. Fraser then orders a full stop, and waits.

Rahe also waits. He decides to play a game of cat and mouse and orders a course for due south. Then he decides to surface as a tease to the Canadian boat.

Fraser, instinctively sensing the sub's movements, orders the *Waskesiu* to 10, then 15 knots, preparing for a full-pattern attack. Contact is lost again. Fraser decides on a bold attack course. He puts himself in the place of the German commander and orders the *Waskesiu* to surge ahead, dropping a pattern of charges well in advance of where he believes his target is heading.

The sub bumps into the explosions, and the force tosses the U-boat around like a plastic boat in a child's bath. A few rivets pop and small leaks trickle ominously down the corners, reminding the crew of how vulnerable they are to the sea around them. The German commander changes his orders to surface and curses softly, sending the sub deeper to avoid rather than play with the *Waskesiu*. These Canadians are proving to be more of a challenge than he had expected. It is time to lay low.

On the surface, Fraser continues to hunt around the area until he regains contact on the asdic. With heightened adrenaline, he orders another full 10 charge attack on the sub. Whumph! The boat tosses and then leaps with the recoil. Silence ...

The Canadians search the water for signs of wreckage, but there is nothing. All attention is focused on the asdic. It is very quiet, the crew is listening intently for the "ping" that says their prey is still there. Fraser orders a cup of kye to settle his nerves, and balances the cup on his knee as he contemplates the situation. He knows the sub is there, he simply has to find her. Using the flare still burning on the water's surface as a starting point, he orders a box search of the area, closely monitoring the asdic. At 3:27 a.m., the *Waskesiu* is again in pursuit, and attack after attack is launched. Plumes of frothy white ocean are sent up into the dark sky with each blast.

Commander Birch, in the *Nene*, rushes to join the battle. He orders Captain Fraser to stand down (to stand aside or give over) so the *Nene* can locate the U-boat. Fraser sighs, and the *Waskesiu* waits, slowly circling. The crew crowds to the sides of the deck, and can faintly see and smell oil floating on the waves.

"Too easy," Fraser thinks to himself. He wonders if this is a simple ruse. U-boats often discharge items mixed with fuel to throw off the hunter. The *Waskesiu* anxiously waits for the arrival of the *Nene*, afraid the prey will escape while they are stuck waiting.

At 4:10 a.m. the *Nene* makes contact. The *Waskesiu* is idling along at only five knots. The sub is moving slowly northeast, and is very deep. W.A. Fogg sends the signal to the *Nene*. And the *Nene* orders Fraser to follow the sub's movements closely but to wait until daylight before attacking.

A short time later, the *Nene* decides the blip on the asdic is a whale and not a U-boat. Birch orders the *Waskesiu* to abandon the hunt and rejoin the convoy. "You're chasing shadows, man," Birch signals them. But Fraser trusts his navigator, Lieutenant Williams, who is monitoring the asdic. Fraser asks Birch for permission to make one more attack. Reluctantly, Birch agrees.

Increasing the speed to 10 knots, Fraser orders a deep depth-charge pattern, then changes the order to semi-deep at the last second and increases speed. Whumph! The *Waskesiu* jumps as explosions rock the frigate. Spouts of water reach high into the air and the crew cheers.

Commander Rahe in the U-boat curses angrily. The damn Canadians are too close, damaging the main engines and causing leaks in the control and engine room. Rahe orders the boat to the surface and swings about to ram the frigate, but finds his engines sluggish and unresponsive.

The *Waskesiu* hears the sub blowing tanks as it hits the surface. Fraser orders the gun armament to prepare to fire and increases speed until the U-boat is spotted on the port bow. "Starshell!" orders Fraser, and the sky is lit up with flares suspended by parachutes, which drift slowly down to the waves. In the light the U-boat is plainly visible. She lists to one side and starts to sink.

The *Nene* receives the coded message "Hearse Is Parked" just before the *Waskesiu* closes in and opens fire. The two Bren guns on her bridge fire 170 rounds while, on the forecastle, bursts from a machine gun pierce the early morning light. Thomas Stephenson, on the No. 1 Oerlikon gun, focuses on the sub's conning tower to prevent any of the Germans from making it to the guns in one piece.

The submarine crosses the *Waskesiu*'s bow about 100 metres away, and passes slowly down her port side, which is now illuminated by searchlights on the frigate. The U-boat is so close that the Canadians are unable to come around fast enough to ram her. The U-boat wallows and Rahe knows it's the sub's death knell. He orders his men to abandon ship. Then Rahe throws his life jacket and dingy to the men in the water — quickly re-enters the sinking U-boat — and closes the hatch firmly behind him.

The U-boat groans and, with a sucking noise, upends and sinks vertically, stern first. The German survivors fight with the waves to escape from the undertow, which is about to pull them down with the sub. Struggling in the bitterly cold Atlantic, they yell out to the Canadians, "Hallo! Hallo! Kamerad!"

The *Nene* and the *Waskesiu* lower their whalers to rescue the submariners who are yelling, blowing whistles, and waving their arms. The *Waskesiu* manages to take aboard only four Germans, hauling them out of the water and over the ship's stern. Using searchlights, the *Nene* is able to rescue another 15 men.

The Germans are well-treated on their way back to England. The four on the *Waskesiu* are given clothing, food, and drink, and they are soon exchanging war stories with the crew. Walter Fogg is happy to accept the Germans' autographs on the back of his HMCS *Waskesiu* official commissioning notice.

Walter Fogg now lives in Selkirk, Manitoba, with his wife. Upon being interviewed, he stated that the Canadians were known for three things during World War II — their marksmanship, their ability to survive the elements, and the humanity they offered a surrendered or wounded enemy.

# Chapter 5
# Bones

he crew isn't aware of it, but the departure, course, and speed of the Canadian destroyer HMCS *Assiniboine*, as well as the convoy, is known to German Admiral Doenitz. When "Bones" (the popular nickname of the *Assiniboine*) joins SC–94 convoy as an escort ship in early August 1942, German submarines are already on a course to intercept.

Lieutenant Commander Lemcke of the *U-210* is ordered to take position as close to the edge of the "black pit" of the Atlantic as possible. Lemcke is the infamous captain who sank a passenger liner at the outbreak of war, breaking the rules laid out by the superpowers giving safe passage for travellers. After hiding out until the furor died down at home, he

The HMCS *St. Thomas,* a Castle Class Corvette

is again ready and able for action. Looking for another notch on his belt, he is anxious for the chance to attack.

The black pit is the area beyond the fuel capacity of the Allied aircraft. Without the benefit of air protection, ships in this area are vulnerable to attack. In view of this problem, the British had come up with the convoy system, using faster, smaller boats as escorts for the lumbering fuel tankers and supply ships. The destroyers, corvettes, and frigates are heavily armed and, while not able to protect all the ships in the group, they definitely are a force to contend with. The U-boat captains all keep a close eye on the escorts while they hunt the fat fuel tankers. The fewer merchant vessels there are that reach port, the more difficult it is for Britain to feed her civilians and her military, and to fuel her military vehicles.

It is late afternoon on August 2. The day is dull and thick patches of fog inch across the ocean. The misty sea air has soaked everything above and below ship on the *Assiniboine*, and in some areas the fog creeps through doorways like smoke. The crew is wearing the best it has for the weather, but even so, there isn't a dry man aboard.

The tension on the escort ships is high, as there is a known wolf pack of U-boats in the area. The ships are staying in close formation and the crews, expecting trouble, are standing by their action stations. The crew on the *Assiniboine* is restless. The fog mutes the sound of the waves slapping against the hull, yet amplifies the throbbing of the engines below deck. The men strain their eyes and ears for the first sign of trouble. They know they are surrounded by at least 30 convoy ships, but the fog has a way of creating a feeling of isolation.

At 6 p.m. on August 3, the lead ship, the *Trehata*, signals a course change, but not everyone receives the order. HMCS *Nasturtium*, HMCS *Orillia*, and six merchantman ships continue on the old course, unknowingly leaving the safety of the group. For two days ships are sent out to locate the missing ones. Finally, on August 5, a radiogram from the *Orillia* reports their position as 33 kilometres south of the main convoy. The *Assiniboine*, one of Canada's River Class Destroyers, is sent to herd the lost sheep and bring them home.

Before anyone can breathe a sigh of relief, the peace is shattered by an explosion. The SS *Spar* is torpedoed by Lieutenant Gerd Kelbling's *U-593* and sinks in minutes. Eleven kilometres away, the *Assiniboine* crew hear and feel the torpedoes exploding the hull of the *Spar*. Escorts race to the location and find debris and pools of oil burning eerily on the surface of the waves. Kelbling fires again at another ship in the convoy. The *Nasturtium* spots the torpedo track and all the ships turn "hard-a-starboard," watching the missiles pass by harmlessly. In retaliation, the *Nasturtium* makes a blind attack with depth charges. Then she lowers her boats to pick up the survivors of the *Spar*. Thirty-six men and the ship's dog are pulled out of the frigid waters while the U–boat sinks deeper to avoid the explosives. At 7:20 p.m., a large splash near the wreckage is spotted, but all the *Assiniboine* can find is bubbles. She stays in the area for a while and then rejoins the convoy.

On the morning of August 6, Canadian Bill Leggett is on the bridge and attending his station as rangefinder director of the *Assiniboine* when the *U-210* is spotted a few kilometres away on the convoy's starboard bow. A break in the fog has blown its cover — a good thing, since the ship's British-fitted 286M radar had failed to detect its presence. Often this type of radar set is referred to by the seamen as "the Jerry's most effective secret weapon."

The *Assiniboine*'s captain, John Stubbs, reports the sighting to the *Primrose* and orders a course straight for the U-boat. The sub hesitates, and then takes off with the

*Assiniboine* hot on its tail. The ship stays starboard of the U-boat. If the *U-210* dives she will be forced to turn to port and the destroyer will have her.

The *Assiniboine* takes aim at the sub's conning tower and fires three salvoes (a direct order to overshoot then under-shoot to determine distance) as she closes in on the enemy. The Germans fly into action with a wild series of manoeu-vres, each one countered by the *Assiniboine*. A deadly game of cat and mouse ensues, with both ships trying to ram the other. The sky is littered with tracer, the destroyer recoils with every gun blast, and dishes go flying in the mess. Anyone who needs to use the head does so at considerable risk of personal injury. Each side is sure of its Atlantic supremacy. The power struggle escalates.

The HMS *Dianthus* is ordered to assist and she explodes on the scene in full throttle. Captain Stubbs swings slightly starboard of his target, opening up the distance for his guns to find aim and to cut off the U-boat's escape route. Meanwhile, the *Dianthus* is closing the gap from behind. The quarters are so close that the *Assiniboine* is unable to fire her 4.7-inch guns, and the U-boat stays close to prevent the Canadians from firing those guns. The Canadians man the mounted Lewis machine gun as well as the one-man guns. The sub fights a stubborn battle, diving to port. She is leak-ing. Oil is streaking the water with pockets of flame floating freely on the swells like splatters of blood. Still, Lemcke fights on, ordering the wounded sub to dive.

The *Assiniboine* and the *Dianthus* start a box search once the sub disappears under the waves. After a few moments the search is called off. No wreckage is found and the asdic is silent. Everyone knows the danger has not passed as there are more U-boats reported in the vicinity. However, they still have a convoy to protect and Stubbs alters to the northeast to rejoin it. The *Assiniboine* is now 21 kilometres ahead, with the *Dianthus* five kilometres off her port beam. The escorts begin a zigzag pattern to cover more ocean in front of the merchant ships once they are again in their convoy position.

Captain Lemcke, after an hour's silence, surfaces his vessel and heads again for the tankers, which are now a few kilometres ahead. He's closely monitoring the destroyers moving restlessly back and forth in front, and eagerly sets his sights for the fat merchant ships inside the escorts' circle.

The *Assiniboine*'s yeoman of signals sights the surfaced U-boat at about a kilometre away, shifting in and out of patches of dense fog. Stubbs turns the destroyer toward the point where the U-boat is last seen and informs the *Dianthus* that the game is not yet over. The two search for over an hour, until the conning tower of the *U-210* is again sighted. Lemcke is lying quietly on the surface, believing the sub is hidden by fog. Seeing the Canadians change course toward him, the German guns his engines and disappears into the fog. A deadly game of hide and seek begins. Whenever the destroyer's 4.7-inch guns are on target, the target disappears in the mist like the ghost ship *Flying Dutchman*. Lemcke seems to be engaged in the battle, laughing with his crew and crawling inside the head of his enemy.

The destroyer speeds up and goes forward, swings around, and comes on the *U-210* unexpectedly from the front. Captain Lemcke is on the bridge. While surprised by the closeness of the destroyer, he chooses to stand his ground. He fancies he is squaring off face-to-face with Stubbs. If he dives, his sub could slip away, but he tells his crew that he can beat the enemy on the surface since it's only a Canadian bucket. How good can these Canadians be? He turns the sub down the port side to get inside the destroyer's turning circle and beneath the aim of her main guns. He plans to swing wide quickly and then ram the destroyer behind the "B" guns. Or at least prevent the *Assiniboine* from firing and ramming him instead.

Stubbs is so close to Lemcke that he swears he can hear the submarine commander breathing. As the sub twists and turns, Stubbs orders the guns to continue firing, more to keep his men busy than with any hope of actually hitting the U-boat. The *U-210* is returning fire bullet for bullet. Shells are whizzing past the heads of the Canadians and, angered by the audacity of the Germans, the gun crews are hammering right back. The distinct smell of explosives and burning cordite is filling the air, the fog drifts around them in damp curls, and the battle takes a personal turn. Which captain will out-manoeuvre the other? Whose crew is more accurate? Which vessel has a sharper turn? Will the Germans' stubbornness win out? As the fog lifts, the two commanding officers watch each other at their respective posts. Almost eye-to-eye, only a few metres apart, they observe each other's movements and try to calculate the other's next move.

Stubbs watches Lemcke give wheel orders, and imagines the smirk on the German's face. Stubbs sets his jaw. A gun crew appears on the deck of the U–boat and makes a run for the forward guns, but the *Assiniboine*'s multiple .5 inch machine guns mow them down, then destroy the forward guns. All that the German crew has left are the machine guns on the bridge. With grim determination they rake the destroyer from stem to stern with a string of burning-hot bullets, setting the ship's flag deck on fire and igniting the fuel tank of the motor launch on the deck below. The *Assiniboine*'s bridge crew race to put out the flames outside the wheelhouse and near the bridge. Meanwhile, Stubbs calmly sits and contemplates the other captain through the smoke. He gives his orders quietly, without emotion, as he stares down Lemcke from across the water.

Lieutenant Commander Lemcke orders his sub closer to the destroyer's side to prevent the *Assiniboine* from ramming the sub. Standing on his small bridge and shouting orders down the voice pipe to his control-room crew, Lemcke knows his vessel's slightest shift in course and speed. It's as if the sub is an extension of his own body. The *Assiniboine* fires a direct hit on the Germans. Jerry fires a direct hit back at the Canadians. Spouts of water rise up from the waves where shells land short or long. Smoke from the fire and the guns drifts on the ocean breeze, filling both sides with determination. German sailors are swept off the U-boat's casing by the destroyer's fire when they try to man their guns. But at the same time, German shells are hailing the *Assiniboine's* bridge and forward guns.

Kenneth Watson is running back and forth, dodging the enemy guns while he diligently supplies round after round of ammo to his gun crew. Suddenly, in a storm of bullets, Watson is hit. He lands hard. Bullets continue to whiz overhead and his blood mixes with the sea water on the deck. Still, he's determined not to let the enemy win. Ignoring the burning in his leg and arm and the blood running into his boot, he picks up his load of ammunition. He delivers the load and turns back to get more. A fresh hail of bullets ping repeatedly onto the metal sheeting behind him, and then thud into his warm body. This time when he hits the deck he doesn't get up again, and the *Assiniboine* loses her youngest crew member.

In that same hail of bullets, Petty Officer Claude Daly is shot in the face. The German bullet passes through his cheek and out of his mouth. Choking on his own blood, his face burning from the wound, he moves Watson's body to one side and continues to carry out his duty. Suddenly, Bill Leggett is sprayed with shrapnel. It splatters over his body and seriously injures one of his arms. He is taken below decks, where the doctor applies a tourniquet. Thirteen others are also wounded. Those unable to continue the fight are moved below decks so they can be treated safely. Others, still wounded, set their jaws with Canadian pride and fight on.

"A" gun's crew has now been reduced to three due to casualties. Able Seamen Stanley Clarke and Morris Young keep the gun firing despite the shelling and the bullets flying over and around them. Able Seaman Roger Whynot can see that the "Y" gun on the *Assiniboine* isn't firing. Although he has no gunnery experience, he and Able Seaman Michael Scullion, as well as one other crew member clean out the jam. Then they load the gun and fire continuously at the U-boat, providing coverage for the fire crews.

The U-boat's guns fire repeatedly and knock out the *Assiniboine*'s main aerial, making it impossible for the destroyer to contact the other ships. Leading Telegraphist Walter Sutherland successfully climbs to the top of the ship and rigs a temporary aerial while ducking German bullets.

The fire is still raging, billows of black smoke and flames obscuring the only entrance to the wheelhouse. The German guns concentrate on that area, hoping to disable the destroyer by blowing out her command post. There is an explosion and flames leap skyward. A member of the *Assiniboine* bridge crew is badly hit. With bullets and shrapnel flying around them and flames licking at the wheelhouse, Sub-Lieutenant Douglas Martin hoists his injured crew mate on his back in a fireman's hold. He climbs through the bullets and flames to the chart house where Surgeon Lieutenant Arnold Johnson has set up the medical station.

Meanwhile, Acting Chief Petty Officer Max Bernays, manning the wheel through all the turns and twists, orders First Lieutenant Ralph Hennessy and a damage-control party to fight the fire. Bernays carries on alone at the wheel. Flames and smoke fill the wheelhouse, making it difficult to see or breathe. At times it appears the fire will rage out of control and consume Hennessy. However, taking his duty to his ship seriously, he chooses to remain alone at his post for the next 40 minutes, doing the work of three men, including dispatching the 133 telegraph orders necessary to effectively battle the U–boat.

The bridge ladders are in flames, so the firefighters climb down the lower mast to reach the upper deck. Gunner Norman Wilkinson is wounded and sent to find medical help below. Seeing the flames, he ignores his injury and joins in the firefighting. Once he and the others climb down, they find Chiefs Don Portree and Charles Burgess already with a firefighting team in action. Portree grabs the nozzle of the fire hose and yells for the water valve to be turned on. The pressure hits with such unexpected force that he is flipped over the rails. Portree holds onto the hose for dear life, water spurting into the air. Other members of the party grab the hose and haul him up the side and onto the deck once more, successfully turning the hose onto the flames.

There is another small explosion and Seaman Norman Leckie leaps through the flames into the sick bay to rescue the medical supplies. Seaman Ed Bonsor leaves his post to help move the wounded out of harm's way. With smoke curling around him he piles hammocks against the ship's side to protect his injured crewmates from stray shrapnel. Above him, Stubbs continues his battle with the U-boat. With the firing of the big guns, the *Assiniboine* leaps with the recoil. Yet the sub seems to go undamaged. For a few moments, it appears the Canadians might lose the battle. Flames are leaping higher around the wheelhouse, and still the destroyer can't get the distance needed to lock onto the target.

Able Seaman John White is the first to locate the sub on radar. Regardless of the activity and fire around him, White is completely focused on his job. He reports the sub's exact location to the captain. Thanks to this information, Stubbs's manouevering is successful. Two shells from the *Assiniboine* hit the U-boat's conning tower, killing every man on the bridge — including Lemcke. Though wounded and badly shaken, the Germans' first watch officer assumes command. He keeps his guns firing at the destroyer, hoping the Canadians will be so busy dodging bullets that the U-boat will be able to slip silently beneath the waves. The German lieutenant gives the order to dive.

Stubbs, seeing that his adversary Lemcke is finished, anticipates the dive. He swings the *Assiniboine* around to ram the wounded vessel. After a couple of tries, he rams the U-boat right behind the conning tower and water pours into the sub. The diesel engines are flooded with sea water. They stall. The *U-210* is dead in the water, bobbing wounded and broken on the waves. It is now at the mercy of the ocean and the Canadians. But the Germans don't give up. With handguns and rifles they pour onto the sub's deck and continue the fight with the destroyer. Seaman Earl Costello grabs a .5-inch machine gun and peppers the sub with bullets, preventing any of the Jerries from reaching their forward guns. Then the *Assiniboine* rams the enemy again. The Germans throw their guns overboard and the battle is over. As soon as the order is given to abandon ship, the Germans scuttle the *U-210*, putting an explosive charge in the periscope shaft before surrendering. With hands raised, the remaining Germans climb up on the sub's deck through the forward hatch. Within two minutes there is an explosion and the sub sinks.

The *Assiniboine* has suffered major damage. Twenty of the crew are injured but, miraculously, only one crew member is dead. Medical Officer Johnstone and Norman Leckie are still working at a frantic pace.

# Chapter 6
# The Sinking of *U-94*, Canadian Style

I t's a balmy August and the year is 1942. There is a lull in the fighting off Iceland. Most of the U-boats are down off the US eastern seaboard. The convoy system of Canada and Britain has proven extremely effective against the U-boats, so the Germans have begun to focus on single American ships, finding them easier targets.

On August 25, the HMCS *Oakville*, a Canadian Flower Class Corvette-K178, zigzags on the port quarter of Convoy TQW-15. She has been ordered on escort duty with two other Canadian corvettes, the HMCS *Snowberry* and the HMCS *Halifax*. The convoy is also escorted by the Dutch *Jan Van Brackel* and by three small patrol craft of the US Navy. The command ship of this escort group is the powerful USS *Lea*, a destroyer.

By August 27 the group is slightly south of Haiti. Germany knows exactly where they are. So does Oberleutnant Otto Ites, commander of *U-94*. Ites is 24 years old and has served four years in U-boats. He has already sunk over 100,000 tons of shipping in this war and is thirsty for more. Back in April, Adolf Hitler had awarded him the Knight's Cross of the Iron Cross. He is proud of his accomplishments and is a challenging adversary. Ites is admired by his crew as a fighter and is personally well-liked. They call him "Onkel Otto." The Allies have other names for him, and no captain in a merchant ship wants to know that the Onkel is tracking his ship across the ocean.

On August 28, 1942, with only the sub's conning tower visible, Ites is stalking the convoy, closing the gap at deadslow speed off their port bow. Gebeschus, his executive officer, is on the bridge with him. Ites quietly assesses the three escort ships, which are pacing restlessly back and forth in front of those tantalizing tankers he has crept four kilometres to destroy. He can taste the victory and yearns to see smoke and flames billowing skyward. Ites decides that by sneaking around the edge of the leading corvette, the HMCS *Snowberry*, he will have a clear target. Another ship to add to his list of kills.

It's a clear night, with a tropical wind force of four — residue from an earlier squall. Whitecaps are still apparent, and while the storm has all but blown itself out, the sea is still very rough. Most of the crews on the Canadian ships are lightly clad due to the humidity and those sleeping below decks have stripped down to their shorts. The HMCS *Oakville*'s first lieutenant, K.B. Culley, keeps his eyes on the surface whitecaps in the heavy swell. There is no reason to expect trouble but he senses the nearby sub and keeps a diligent watch for a telltale periscope.

Ites in the *U-94* estimates the convoy's speed at about 10 knots and orders an intercept course, decreasing speed to three knots. He decides that the tankers would be easy targets for his torpedoes, if it wasn't for the weaving *Snowberry*. Ites watches the escorts' movements and realizes that the *Snowberry* and the *Oakville* are zigzagging in tandem. And the *Snowberry* is staying on one leg of the zigzag for at least three minutes. He calculates the *Snowberry*'s next turn and cuts as close to the corvette as possible. He plans on slipping into the gap between the two Canadian ships, swinging around once clear, then firing on the fully loaded tankers.

Ites decides to ignore the small US Navy patrol craft darting between the escort ships, since it is a small threat. So intent is he on the corvettes and the manoeuvres around his intended targets, Ites doesn't see the US Navy's Catalina circling in the air above. But the pilot sees the U-boat. Its conning tower is in the silver path of the moon's light, looking black and threatening against the ocean. The aircraft circles and dives in quickly. The pilot knows a U-boat only needs 30 seconds to dive, so surprise is his best bet.

## The Sinking of U-94, Canadian Style

"Bombs away!" the order is yelled. Pulling up and away, the Catalina banks to watch the show. Ites curses when he hears the engines of the aircraft above and sees the bomb doors open in silent slow motion. As death drops from above, Onkel orders the *U-94* to dive, but it is too late. The bombs explode in a perfect straddle, three charges on both sides of the conning tower. The *U-94*'s stern is blown high into the air, destroying her aft diving planes, which keep the U-boat level while on top of the water. Like a stranded fish gasping for air, the U-boat flounders for a moment in the waves as the victorious aircraft drops marker flares. The *U-94*, despite her wounds, continues to dive.

Sub-Lieutenant Graham Scott is the officer of the watch on the *Oakville*'s bridge. He hears the explosions as columns of white froth erupt into the night sky. He yells down the pipe, "Action stations!" And Lieutenant Commander Clarence King immediately orders full speed ahead and alters course toward the flares. The little *Oakville* jumps on top of the waves and races after the enemy.

The urgent jangle of the action-station bells on the *Oakville* jerks the crew from sleep, but the pitching of the ship under full engines ahead makes it difficult for them to rush up to the deck to their battle stations. Those who try to get into battle dress quickly give up the struggle and land on deck in whatever attire they were wearing to bed. Swarming up the ladder, the bridge crew push and shove past each other. There's a battle, and all of them want in on the action.

71

First Lieutenant Lawrence bursts into the asdic shack in time to see Leading Seaman Hartman shoving the cruising watch operator out of the seat and taking his place at the headset. All that can be seen of the plumes of water from the aircraft's depth-bombs is a rainbow mist in the moonlight. The last of the black conning tower is disappearing below the surface. Hartman swings the transmitter to the bearing of the depth-bombs' splashes. Ping ... sounds the oscillator. The sonar searches outward, the sound waves are coming back fainter and fainter.

Hartman swings his set to the right. Ping ... again, then the echoes fade. He swings his set to the left, trying to get a steady bead on the German sub below them. The aircraft above is using Morse code flashes in the night sky with a signal light. The pilot is watching the shadow of the black death as it descends to the ocean depths, and is letting all the ships know where the threat is headed. A lone marking flare drifts down in the night sky, and more than 100 sets of eyes watch it intently. The crew holds their breath and waits minutes that seem years long. Below them hides a U-boat, stalking the convoy. With their noses to the air, faces to the wind, the Canadians are waiting too, waiting for the wolf to pounce and give away his location.

"Fire a five-charge pattern when we cross the spot where those depth-bombs landed." The captain's quiet orders on the *Oakville* break the silence. Lieutenant Commander Clarence King had won a Distinguished Service Cross in World War I for sinking one U-boat and getting two probable kills. He's anxious for his first kill in this war, and, as all the great Canadian captains do, he attempts to think like the commander on the sub. He glances nervously over the waves toward the rest of the convoy. In his mind he sees the distance and location of each ship, and pictures the U-boat under the water. Which tanker will it go for first?

King orders a drop of five depth charges set to 30 metres. Whompff! ... The ship jumps, recoiling from the release of the explosives. The engines are gunned and the *Oakville* leaps on top of the waves to put distance between her and the charges. King knows he's shooting in the dark, and he knows that the charges will probably only keep the sub down. But if the sub stays down then the tankers are safe for the time being, as the sub needs to surface to fire torpedoes. Of course, no one will be totally safe until that German U-boat is put to rest for good.

The *Oakville*'s asdic is silent. The crew tenses, hearts beating as one. With a rumble the bombs explode. Water erupts to masthead height as the *Oakville* bucks, lurches, and trembles. The crew jumps into action like a well-oiled machine. King feels the hull groan and twist and mentally he strokes his ship. "Easy, girl," he whispers in the dark.

Hartman is sweeping for contact on the asdic, trying to ignore the activity and focus on his task. He swings to the right — ping. Before the reverberations die out there is a low drumming note in Hartman's earphones — the throb of turbines. He stands up and intuitively swings the oscillator further to the right. He breaks into a huge grin. The low drumming in his earphones changes to a clamour as the submarine blows her ballast tanks. The *U-94* is surfacing. "We've got her!" Hartman yells. "The bugger is surfacing! The chase is on!"

The captain smiles. "There's the bastard!" he shouts. The black snout of the U-boat rears out of the boiling water ahead with water cascading off her deck as she swings left. The conning tower slices through a swell, glimmering ethereally in the silver moonlight. The Canadians feel a collective shiver and then brace for the spring.

King swings the corvette around to ram the sub. Rivets pop and the hull strains in a curve so tight the crew thinks King must ride motorcycles on land. "Load and fire starshell!" the captain commands. Flares light up the night sky, prompting the escorts to madly gather together the convoy. They know the flare means a U-boat is in the vicinity and they group their herd and move them out of harm's way.

King orders his first lieutenant to prepare to ram the U-boat and to get ready to shore-up the bulkheads after the impact. The submarine manoeuvres to pass closely under the ship's bow, to prevent being rammed. King has other ideas. "Hard-a-port!" he yells, racing the Germans for the turning space. But the sub arrives there first, and with only 30 metres to manoeuvre in, the *Oakville* can't make the turn. King curses. The *U-94* crashes down the port side of the Canadian corvette, grinding and bouncing off the hull. Onkel shakes his head at the determination of the small craft.

The Canadian crew lets fly the bullets at the bow of the submarine. King alters to starboard to once again try to widen the gap for ramming, and to give the guns room to fire. The guns roar out again and again, spitting fire and explosives at the German threat. The crew cheers above the booming of the guns and the throbbing of the engines. A shell explodes on the conning tower of the sub and the Canadians' enthusiasm grows.

The red tracer increases from the *Oakville*, ricocheting at wild angles off the thick hull of the *U-94*. Machine guns add to the cacophony and small arms begin firing at the U-boat, preventing the Germans from manning any of their guns. The corvette's bow swings around again. Ites knows what's coming and orders a turn to counter the *Oakville*'s swing into a ramming position. Onkel can't believe the bull-dog tenacity of this small ship, trying time after time to ram the German steel without fear for her own safety.

Increasing the sub's speed, Ites dodges the corvette's movements yet again. He passes to the starboard of the *Oakville* under a hail of bullets. With precision and speed, the German gunners pour out of the forward hatch and make for their weapons. They are picked off one by one. The Canadians focus their attention on the Germans' 88mm deck gun. The gun starts to wiggle, then it rocks, and smoke starts to curl around it. Finally it topples into the water with a splash, followed by the cheering of the *Oakville* crew. But Ites manoeuvres the *U-94* with skill, gaining speed away from the corvette.

King gives chase in a rivet-popping, hull-bending turn that sends everything that is not tied down careening below like unguided missiles. Dishes smash and men hang on for dear life. Gaining momentum, the *Oakville* rams the U-boat, striking her a glancing blow on the starboard side. The *U-94* passes six metres off and down the port side of the corvette.

Stationed behind the ship's smokestack, six stokers who have not had a part in this battle decide that watching is just not good enough. Dragging out a box of glass pop bottles, the men start yelling curses at the Germans, who are only feet away. They throw the empties at the U-boat. In shock, the Germans stare at these madmen and duck. They're too stunned to shoot at the bottle throwers but are forced to avoid the glass that is smashing onto the deck of their sub.

King orders an additional depth charge and this one explodes directly under the *U-94*. The sub bucks and tosses about like a bull at a rodeo. For a few seconds the ocean spray obscures her from view, splattering the *Oakville* with salty foam. The U-boat slows and wallows in the kicking surf. King orders the corvette to swing out, and the *Oakville* revs her engines and leaps forward, ramming the U-boat squarely behind the conning tower. The corvette's bow rears up with the impact and she cries out from the wound. The *U-94* rolls uselessly in the waves. Beneath the bottom of the ship, the *Oakville* feels three distinct shocks, and the vessel jars. A ripping of metal is heard throughout the ship as the sub gashes the *Oakville*'s hull. The No. 2 boiler room on the little

corvette and the lower asdic compartment both flood. The
crew struggles to get the flooding under control.

The *U-94* wallows astern and stops, sloshing backwards
and forwards. Both vessels are severely damaged. The guns
continue to send a steady stream of fire, with bullets winging
off the sub at wild angles. Tracer is glowing white-hot in an
uninterrupted stream.

The battle isn't over yet. King intends to capture the
U-boat and orders a landing party on board the floundering submarine. Obediently, the men slide down the ladder
and scramble for their gear. Seaman Harold Lawrence, in
his haste to join the battle, is clothed only in his life belt
and underwear.

When the 12 crew members muster on the port side
the gun is silent as they prepare to leap onto the deck of the
crippled submarine. The party thinks that the *Oakville's* gun
has been silenced for their leap, but in fact the gun has mis-
fired and First Lieutenant Culley is trying to clear the jam.
He discharges the shell, throws it over the side, reloads, and
swings the muzzle over close to Lawrence's right ear — just
as Lawrence and Powell are leaning over the rail preparing to
leap. One startled look over their shoulders at the sound of
the gun swivelling, and the boarding party scuttles for safety.
"Fire!" Whompff! The ship jumps with recoil.

The blast blows Lawrence and Powell onto the deck
below. Momentarily stunned, they get back up, and in spite
of bleeding noses and bruises, they spring into the air and

onto the heaving German submarine. The waistband on Lawrence's underwear snaps on impact. Stunned by the shell blast, he kicks his shorts off and stands naked and glowing white in the moonlight. Lawrence and Powell are the only two who make it onto the sub. Suddenly a wave surges over the casing, washing Lawrence over the side. Powell reaches out and grabs him by the life belt, dragging him back onto the deck of the sub.

The crew of the *Oakville*, highly excited by the frenzy of the battle, rain a hail of bullets on the sub from one end to the other. They don't realize they're shooting at their own crew members. Lawrence and Powell dive for cover. The bullets ricochet off the metal deck with a whizzing clunking sound while the pair, keeping as low as possible, make for the bridge. Powell wears a proud grin, Lawrence is wearing only a life belt.

Suddenly, a German steps out from behind the forward gun and pauses for a second at the sight of the two Canadians. Pumped with adrenaline, Lawrence hits him with his pistol barrel and knocks him into the waves. Rounding the conning tower, they're confronted by two more Germans emerging from the hatch below. The Canadians rush forward, surprising the enemy in more ways than one. One German takes a horrified look at Lawrence's lack of clothing and instantly jumps into the smashing sea. Powell rushes the other and kicks him over the side to join his shocked crew mate, who is treading water close to the doomed U-boat.

## The Sinking of U-94, Canadian Style

Soon the two lone Canadians find themselves surrounded by 26 Germans, all pouring out from below. The Canadians have the only pistols, but only one Canadian has clothes on. At this point, even with the guns, Lawrence begins to feel he's at a disadvantage. He debates whether or not to borrow a German uniform, but he dismisses the idea as unpatriotic.

Powell herds the submariners to the after gun-platform, which is pocked by bullet holes. The forward end of the bridge is crumpled from the ramming and the hatch is stuck open at about 50 degrees. Lawrence slides over a body, wriggles underneath the hatch, and drops down into the guts of the U-boat to see if anything can be salvaged. It is a waste of time, as the Germans have already scuttled the dying U-boat and destroyed its important papers. Lawrence climbs back out. The U-boat rolls, then rolls again, and the watertight bulkhead gives way as Lawrence quickly orders everyone into the water. The *U-94* sinks a short time later.

The USS *Lea* is combing the area looking for survivors and is signalled by King to rescue the boarding party as well. King is now temporarily stopped by the *Oakville*'s flooded engine room, and is on minimal power. The *Lea* collects 21 Germans.

Lawrence is pulled from the water, still wearing only his life belt. The American crew aren't sure if he is German or Canadian. Quickly, Lawrence resorts to some salty Canadian slang to convince his American rescuers that he is from the *Oakville* and not part of the U-boat's crew.

"We figured you had to be Canadian," one seaman responds. "No self-respecting German would ever be caught out of uniform."

The *Oakville* sends out a dinghy to pick up Petty Officer Powell along with five German prisoners. Oberleutnant Otto Ites has three bullet wounds, but he is one of the rescued. Nineteen of the German crew are never found.

No injuries are reported from the flying bottles.

Lawrence is issued a new uniform.

# Chapter 7
# Tribal Kill

The naval grapevine talks about the Tribal Class Destroyers as being slow and under-gunned. The crews of the HMCS *Haida* and the HMCS *Athabaskan* don't agree. The Tribals, they argue, have more guns than River Class Destroyers, and at least seven times the firepower of an ordinary destroyer, if not more. They are often referred to as pocket cruisers, and by the end of World War II, the *Haida* is one of the most celebrated ships in Canadian history. Lieutenant Commander Henry "Harry" George De Wolf is the commander of the *Haida*, and John Stubbs (previously the captain of the *Assiniboine*) is now commanding the *Athabaskan*.

The ships' companies come from every province in Canada. As each new recruit arrives on board, a familiar cry is heard. "Anyone here from the west?" And in salty language someone answers, telling him what they think of the west. A similar query is raised about the east, and again a strong voice yells out what they can do with the east. A good-natured argument then breaks out, and the air buzzes with typical seamen's banter, as friends recognize friends and homesick Canadians compare hometowns and talk of loved ones.

The Tribals are more than just fighting ships to the homesick Canadians. These ships are the saltys' homes, and they're run like a village. All on board put the ship first, their mates second, and themselves last — in true Canadian naval tradition.

The mascot on the *Athabaskan* is a ginger cat who walked up the gangplank one sunny afternoon and has run the ship from that day forward — as only a cat can do. The ship's crew have named her "Ginger," of course. And, although they call her a she, Ginger is a he.

On the *Haida*, the mascot is a small scruffy terrier-like dog with a wet tongue and a wagging tail. The gun crew picked him out from a litter while on shore leave, once they got the okay from the officer of the day (ODO) for a "purebred Airedale pup." The pup is anything but a purebred. However the ODO, himself a dog-lover, tweaked the pup's ear and agreed to have him on board in spite of his dubious parentage. The pup quickly let the ship's two ducks and Angora rabbit know who's boss.

One afternoon, as the *Haida* was being refuelled at

sea, the hose from the tanker that was fuelling bunker "B" came loose. Oil fuel sprayed high in the air and covered the deck and the dog in a black sticky mess. The ship's doctor scrubbed up the wretched animal, and the dog was given the name "Bunker B."

Now, as the ship is standing by, Bunker B (still in late puppyhood) stands with his head cocked to one side, growling at his favourite toy, a leather glove. He is getting saltier every day; he stands completely still during inspection, and knows to bark aggressively at the officers. The gun crew are his gods and he follows them faithfully.

The HMCS *Haida* is part of the 10th Destroyer Flotilla, referred to as Force 26. The ships in this group are the cruiser *Black Prince* and the Canadian Tribal Destroyers *Haida*, *Huron*, and *Athabaskan*, as well as the British destroyer HMS *Ashanti*. Force 26 is one ship short, as the *Tartar* is under a refit. The remaining ships are at port waiting for orders.

Shortly after tea, the captain's sea boat comes alongside the *Haida*. Captain De Wolf climbs up the ladder and retires to his quarters. "Cooks to the galley" is piped earlier than usual, confirming a rumour of an upcoming mission. All hands eat an early supper at 5:30 p.m. The time for sleeping and relaxation is over now. Throughout the ship there is a quiet sense of preparation against the night that is approaching. This is the final harbour hour, and many spend it writing letters home.

"Special sea duty men" is piped at 6:45 p.m., and "Hands fall in" is piped 10 minutes later. The waiting is over.

Each division lines up on deck. The captain climbs up to the bridge, dressed in his sea gear. With a quiet command, the mooring to the buoy is slipped. As the ship swings, obedient to her engines and rudder, she turns down harbour. The sea boat, still alongside, is hooked onto a rope hanging down from hinged booms davits (hinged booms) and is swung up and hoisted on board. As her crew climbs out onto the main deck, the davits are swung inboard and snugged down.

It's always an interesting passage going out from Plymouth. The waterway is narrow, with the shores very close. Sea birds wheel above. Those on board watch the people walking along the shore, a few wave, and the seamen wave back.

The *Haida* passes the signal station, a low, flat-roofed structure perched on a hilltop. The hands come to attention as the pipe for "Still" sounds, and then the men on deck stand easy as the ship motors swiftly by. Bunker B stands still, too, and only his lip curls when the officer walks by. The officer frowns at the dog. The gun crew hide their smiles.

The wind is freshening now as they near the seagate (an anti-submarine net across the harbour suspended by cables). Boats patrol outside the gates and all vessels are checked before the nets are rolled back to allow access to the harbour. Over to port, behind the net, the waiting cruiser slips her moorings to escort them through.

Clear of the seagate, the crew look to catch their last glimpse of the harbour. Each man tries not to think of this being their last sight of "home," but the thought is never too far from their minds. The sunset lights the rooftops and windows with the last colours of the day. Soon England, blacked out for war, will be nothing more than a lump of darkness. Ahead of the ships are the blackened seas of the wind-whipped Channel and the enemy coastline.

The night's work begins and the crew are suddenly too busy to think of shore. Guns and ammunition are checked and re-checked. The Kaaa-thump! of the pom-pom is heard as it opens fire. Then the Oerlikon gunners, targeting the bursts of the pom-pom shells in the evening skies, open fire with tracer on the English side of the Channel. Soon they will be crossing too close to the enemy lines for such attention-drawing displays.

The deadlights on the ships are screwed down on portholes. Hatches are closed and thick canvas curtains are drawn into place across all openings to the deck as the ship travels in blackout conditions. Every man off duty heads below to sleep. When action stations are sounded at 10:30 p.m. they know there will be no rest for any of them until dawn.

Force 26 sails southward across the Channel toward the French coast. "Give me a hand chum," says a westerner to Able Seaman Norman Goodale as he attempts to get a lammy coat (a large overcoat) over his bulky life jacket. It's a tough task under the best of conditions, but the sea air is damp tonight and the lammy keeps sticking to the life jacket. Heavy underwear, thick socks, sweaters, life jackets, ear protectors, anti-flash hoods, steel helmets, lammy coats, and other paraphernalia are being shrugged and strapped on by all the crew. This is for warmth and not meant to be worn in case of a dumping in the ocean. However, warmth is necessary and in the case of an emergency most of this will be easily and quickly peeled away.

Bunker B dances around the men of the *Haida* while they get ready. Red tells him to stay in his bed and keep out of trouble. The men have already made him a hammock, and they promise to find him a life jacket and a helmet when they find the time. Bunker B doesn't understand the words, but he wiggles and wags and drools over the attention.

The buzzers sound their insistent clamour throughout the ship. "Show time," Able Seaman Norman Goodale announces to anyone within earshot. At first Bunker B refuses to be left behind as the hands climb out to the dark decks. Red grabs the dog and hands him over to a rating (a seaman) to confine in a safe place. "Keep him in the Transmitting Station, chum," he requests, "and keep him safe."

Along the decks men are moving swiftly. Magazine hatches are opened, fire-control squads close hatches to sections that will not be in use, and the ship is readied for action. Tensions increase, and men watch the waves nervously.

Up on the bridge the captain, the action officer of the watch, the signalmen, and the gunnery, torpedo, and observer officers are all alert and ready. The captain is the only man who seems calm, sipping a cup of the infamous kye. The different stations all over the ship report to the bridge crew that all is secure and ready. The captain gives the stand-by order and, as they close in on the enemy coastline, the small force of Allied ships is alert and on guard.

Visibility is good, about three-and-a-half kilometres. It's a dark, moonless night, which is ideal for keeping a low profile, but makes it difficult to keep track of the other ships in the group. The *Haida*, with the *Athabaskan* close astern, forms the starboard sub-division of Force 26. The *Black Prince* is on their port side, with the *Huron* and the *Ashanti* forming the port sub-division a bit farther afield.

At 1:00 a.m. a shore light is sighted along the coast of France. Ten minutes later a shore searchlight is spotted from the Ile de Batz lighthouse, raking the dark sky with its ominous beam. "Must be looking for planes," remarks the navigator to no one in particular. A while later, a flash of gunfire is seen, but so far there is no indication that the Canadian ships have been spotted. A few minutes later, another shore light and more flashes of gunfire. The senior officer in the cruiser orders a course change to put more ocean between the ships and the enemy coast.

Ping ... Ping ... Ping ... ships appear on radar and they are heading right for Force 26. "Increase speed to 30 knots for intercept!" the captain orders, and the *Haida* and the *Athabaskan* rev the turbines to close in on the enemy destroyers. The German destroyers head full-speed away and the chase eastward begins. Stokers and engine-room artificers are kept busy, and the throbbing increases as the ships cut through the waves. Excitement replaces anxiety. The order for action stations sounds, and gun crews wait impatiently for the order to open fire. The ammunition hoists below decks are loaded and ready, and with the engines providing a battle cry, the warriors are all in place.

The sharp crack of the *Black Prince* cruiser's gun spits flame and breaks the darkness first. Starshell burst above in an umbrella of white stars, illuminating the enemy at 4000 metres. The destroyers rush the enemy at full speed, and the hum of the turbines rises to a scull-cracking whine as the ships race through the seas. The *Haida* moves in fast with the *Athabaskan* close astern. Ginger the cat has found a nice perch on the bridge of the *Athabaskan* to watch the action, and the crew see it as a good omen.

The Canadian Tribals' job is to engage the enemy, and the *Haida*'s bridge crew searches the seas intently after the starshell bursts. The Germans have laid a smoke screen, cutting down visibility in the dark night. Cautiously, the destroyers close in. Whoompff! The enemy opens fire. Starshell of their own breaks the dark of the night, and shells whiz overhead, sploshing in the cresting seas on the far side of the two Canadian ships.

"Shoot to the left! To the left!" signals the *Haida* to the *Black Prince*, and the cruiser corrects the range and fires starshell again, high into the air. There's a tense moment and the starshell bursts again, flooding the horizon with an eerie light.

"There they are! There they are!" And dotted black against the horizon are three, possibly four, enemy destroyers travelling east under a smoke screen. The time is 2:26 a.m.

"Open fire!" says the captain. "Commence! Commence! Commence!" Well-oiled hoists slam into place, loaded with ammunition as the hatches below the guns are opened.

"Load! ... Load! ... LOAD!!" Whoomff! Fire leaps from the muzzle of the gun as the *Ashanti* jerks from the recoil. It's a hit on the left-hand German ship. Whoomff! Another hit. The *Black Prince* opens fire from "A" turret, while continuing to use "B" turret for starshell to keep the fleeing Germans within sight. The pungent smell of cordite mingles with the night air as the *Haida* opens fire with "A" and "B" guns. As the ship heels with the recoil, the crew are sure they can feel the hull bend from the power of their guns.

The track of the four shells from the *Haida*'s two forward guns blazes a bright trail in the night sky. The bridge crew watch in fascination as the shells arch across the expanse of ocean toward the enemy ships. The *Black Prince* is now firing steadily, and so are the *Haida, Huron, Ashanti*, and *Athabaskan*. The enemy ships turn around and open fire on Force 26. The sounds of whizzing shells and spattering ocean fill the air, punctuated by the return fire from the Canadian ships as they close in on the enemy. The German destroyers swing away and open up their engines to find refuge behind their smoke screen.

"A hit! A hit!" the crews on the Allied ships yell as a glow of flame bursts on an enemy ship, visible even through the smoke. A second hit is spotted on another enemy ship. The Tribals race full-speed ahead, straight at the enemy. Suddenly, the sky turns black as the "B" gun turret on the *Black Prince* becomes silent. The Allied ships are too close. The cruiser swings seaward to clear herself. The Germans take advantage of the break and fire a number of torpedoes. The captain of the *Black Prince* orders hard-a-port, and a torpedo passes on her starboard side. More torpedoes are sighted and the *Black Prince* shoots north full-speed ahead to avoid being hit.

De Wolf, on the *Haida*, is now in command of the destroyers. Illumination is ordered from the *Athabaskan* for the *Haida*, and from the *Ashanti* for the *Huron*. All four ships continue shelling the Germans.

At 3:00 a.m., the enemy destroyers finally emerge from their smoke screen for a moment, and dive back into it again. The *Haida* signals to everyone to watch for torpedoes. Following the contour of the coastline as close as possible, the *Haida* and the *Athabaskan* find themselves close to the enemy's smoke screen. As the coastline veers south, they pull ahead of the *Huron* and the *Ashanti*. Shore batteries open up and the *Huron* and the *Ashanti* are soon engaged while all four Tribals continue firing on the enemy ships ahead. The two groups close in and the fight becomes personal, heightening to a ship-on-ship battle.

The Germans run, ducking right through a known minefield and the Tribals follow them with teeth-clenching determination. Up ahead are the islands of Sept Iles. Tense and alert, the *Haida*'s bridge crew watch for the Jerries' next move. The navigator is keeping a close eye on the charts for sunken rocks close to the shore. Shore batteries are hammering away, so the captains of the ships keep their vessels just out of reach. Navigators are worth their weight in gold during battles such as this. Without their keen eyes, concentration, and ability to ignore the booming guns and the battle all around them, ships could easily land helplessly on rocks.

Up ahead, the smoke screen looks as if it's thinner. As the crews of the Tribals watch, they catch a glimpse of something at the edge of the smoke screen that looks like a ship attempting to double-back. It's a fleeting glimpse, followed by a pause in shooting. The *Haida* takes a chance and darts closer, altering course for her "X" gun mounting to fire starshell. Whoompff! The ship jumps. Well-aimed, the first burst falls directly over and behind the target, casting a shadow of the ship on the cloud of smoke like shadow puppets on a sheet.

Streaking out, clear of the smoke screen, a German destroyer makes a run for it, trying to come around behind the Canadians and pin them between the guns of their other ships. A German Ebling (E-boat) turns broadside to the *Haida* and attacks, giving the other German ships a clear path. The *Haida* signals a 90 degree turn to starboard, ordering the other two Tribals to keep the Germans contained while the *Athabaskan* and the *Haida* turn to face the enemy. The *Haida*'s guns swing and aim steadily on the target up ahead.

The bridge crew of the *Athabaskan* watches intently as the drama of the moment unfolds before them in the eerie light of the starshell mixing with drifting smoke. One moment the enemy is in plain view, speeding along, then the *Haida's* guns crash with salvo after salvo, hiding the night sky and filling the sea breeze with the stench of explosives. There's smoke. There's confusion. There are flames shooting from the guns ...

The first series of shells is a direct hit, catching the E-boat amidships, about three metres below her main deck. The plates crumple like tinfoil. The explosives carve their path through the steel, exploding inside the guts of the ship. A shell crashes aft below deck level, another below the bridge, and finally one smashes into her behind the first.

Great geysers of steam rise from the enemy destroyer amidships. She slows and stops. Red tongues of fire leap into the sky from where the shells hit, quickly exploding into a blazing inferno on her main deck.

The *Athabaskan's* shells are also smashing through the bows and fires break out there as well. Across the flame-lit expanse of water between the Canadian ships and the burning German destroyer, only a few metres away, the Canadians can hear the roar and hiss of escaping steam. The Tribals circle, closing in for the kill.

Meanwhile, the *Huron's* and the *Ashanti's* prey has escaped, so they turn around to join the battle. A group of survivors attempt to escape the burning E-boat on a life raft, but with German guns still being fired at the Tribals, the *Haida* has no choice but to continue the battle. A salvo, intended to strike below the waterline, crashes into the enemy's crippled hull and sends the raft and the men hurtling skyward. It sobers the crew, and while they pause their barrage on the enemy, the German guns jump to life again. The bullets whiz overhead, causing the Canadians on deck to duck. Finally, the enemy guns fade out and only the roar and crackle of the flames can be heard from the E-boat. The silhouettes of Force 26 show like black shadows against the fire-lit horizon.

As the Tribals circle, high on the bridge of the mortally wounded German ship, a lone gunner lets off a few more rounds. Streaking across the narrow gap, the tracer sweeps along the *Haida*'s length. Shooting from a position amidships, with flames dancing around him and shells whizzing past, the lone German gunner makes a gallant last stand, forcing the men on the Tribals to take cover. His shells hit the *Huron*'s bridge and upper rigging, smashing the port navigation lights and the port side of the stoker's mess. Another shell shoots away the pom-pom feed rail, killing Leading Seaman Gosnell on the *Athabaskan* and injuring four others.

Shore batteries open up on the group once again, but the *Black Prince* returns their fire, forcing them to cease. The guns of the Tribals fire repeatedly at the wreck, with a stream of coloured tracer zipping along the enemy's decks, ricocheting over her bridge and after structure. The guns on the E-boat, later identified as T-29s, finally lie silent. The lone gunner lies silent as well.

The Tribals close in for the final sinking. Shell after shell rips into the dead ship, sending up showers of sparks against the black masses of oily smoke billowing in the night. The white clouds of the smoke screen are replaced with a black cloud of death, and here and there on the darkened swells of the ocean, are a few scattered pools of brightly burning fuel. The Tribals alter course again for another round. But then, as they watch, the Ebling rolls to port. Her bow dips, and the fires sizzle, smoke, and sputter as she slips swiftly under the sea. From the *Haida's* foredeck comes the sound of hoarse cheering as the gun crews watch her go. It's 4:20 a.m. Norman Goodale and the rest of the crew are triumphant. And a little sad.

The Tribals catch up to the *Black Prince* at daybreak, and Force 26 sets a course for Plymouth at 25 knots. It has been a successful night's hunting and all the ships sail into the harbour with battle ensigns flying. Several men have suffered minor wounds. Red proudly exhibits a grazed arm and Joe, the lad who intends to marry Sally, has a dented helmet and a bump on the head to show for his night's work. Goodale has escaped injury. And Bunker B? He hid out in the mess during the shooting.

The remaining damaged enemy ships have probably escaped into a protected port along the coast of France. It's a battle for another night, but another night is closer than any of the Tribals suspect.

*Tribal Kill*

The outcome of the battle soon to come will stagger most who witness it, and will be recorded in many history books ...

# Chapter 8
# White and Scarlet,
# "We fight as one"

A s they sail up the harbour the Tribals are scrutinized with interest. The news of their successful battle reaches Plymouth before the ships arrive in port. Once they do arrive, ship after ship salutes them. The crews are happy. The sinking of a German E-boat is a milestone, and the *Athabaskan* and the *Haida* are proud to have been part of it. Bunker B rides on deck with the rest of the *Haida* gun crew, and in celebration, he has a red bandana around his neck.

"Have you dead or injured on board?" the harbour officer calls out.

"We have both," is the answer, and the crew watches in silence as the wounded and dead are taken off the docks by the waiting ambulances.

*White and Scarlet, "We fight as one"*

Dockyard mateys swarm aboard like mother hens to patch the holes that the enemy fire has made in the hull. They tighten the fittings that have been loosened by the vibration of high speeds, as well as the recoil shuddering caused by the firing of the ship's own guns. The crew on the *Haida* mentions the way the ship's hull seemed to bend in the rolling seas. They are told it will be reported and investigated at a later date.

Steam radiators had shaken loose of their fittings and fallen off the walls. Chunks of asbestos had vibrated off overhead pipes. Dishes, which had broken loose from lashed cupboards, lay broken on the decks. Hastily abandoned sea gear litters the deck among the salted swirls of dried sea water. It's a mess to clean up, but it could have been worse. A great deal worse.

Approximately 2100 rounds of ammunition have been fired, and it all needs to be replaced and stored in the proper magazines. Stores are brought on board, damaged equipment replaced, and the fuel bunkers filled. Bunker B watches all this excitement with interest. He seems to think that all the activity is for him as he trots through the soapy water when the ratings wash the deck. Soon the *Athabaskan* and the *Haida* are set to go back to sea.

The night before shipping out, the *Athabaskan* and the *Haida* are in harbour together, both tied to a buoy on which someone has painted "The Canadians." It has been a day of rest, writing letters and playing cards with the crew from the other ship. Late in the afternoon a heavy consignment of mail, parcels, and cigarettes from Canada reaches the ships, and most of the men spend their down time reading the news from home. The cat makes herself at home on both ships. And Bunker finds the gun crew of the *Athabaskan* just as friendly as his own. Time passes quickly until seven o'clock brings the order to slip.

It has been a fine day, a day of sunshine, a day with good company. The crews would have preferred another night in to get caught up on their sleep, but war has its own timetable, so it's grumble and go. The Coastal Forces mine-laying craft will be operating inshore in French waters tonight, and the two Tribals are ordered to watch their backs.

The *Haida* slips the buoy first, turning around and heading for the gate to the Channel. The *Athabaskan* has a little trouble getting clear and scrapes Number 6 Buoy as she swings around. This causes a slight delay, so she increases her speed to catch up. At the seagate the *Haida* slows to pass through. The *Athabaskan* slows and falls in behind.

Down on the quarterdeck a group of officers on the *Haida* are talking. A lieutenant, looking back at the *Athabaskan*, says she'll be lucky, she'll get back all right. He has a premonition of trouble. He figures that the *Haida*, being the lead ship, will draw most of the attention. "There should be more than two of us," grumbles another.

The *Athabaskan* and the *Haida* sail across the Channel as sisters, with a spirit between them that ships of war rarely experience. As they slowly separate before opening up the engines, the *Athabaskan's* cat makes a vain effort to jump aboard the *Haida*. Petty Officers Gerald MacAvoy and John Manson of the *Athabaskan* grab the cat to stop it from falling overboard. Someone says, "That's not a good sign."

"For some strange reason," notes *Haida* petty officer George Goodwill, watching the cat with interest, "it's been coming over to our ship lately, and every time we gently toss it back."

"Not a good sign at all," says Norman Goodale.

Once they are surging across the Channel, all thoughts of foreboding are pushed aside as the ships make ready for the night's operation. They all know D-Day is coming, and hunting U-boats now will make the waters safe for the big invasion. With the lessons of Dunkirk fresh in everyone's mind, the Canadians take their orders very seriously.

When the Tribals arrive on the scene, the mine layers are already underway, using the darkness as cover. The weather is ideal for the operation. There is a clear sky, a waning moon to provide good visibility, and a smooth sea with a gentle swell.

The *Athabaskan*, reflecting the moonlight, looks like a ship of silver as she cruises. She is plainly visible. Like the *Haida*, her crew are ready for action. This is not a new task for the crew; mine laying is a common occurrence. But tonight ... tonight it's different. Call it intuition or a sailor's fancy, but there is something in the air that has the crews of both ships on edge. All are trying not to think of the night of August 27, 1943, when the *Athabaskan* was attacked and hit by 18 enemy Dornier-217s. HMS *Egret*, a British sloop, was sunk that night, and a glide bomb had hit the *Athabaskan*. She managed to sail into port under her own power but with a serious list to starboard. That night wasn't without casualties. And in this war, there are no guarantees.

On the bridge of the *Athabaskan*, Lieutenant Commander Stubbs is discussing battle plans with his first lieutenant, Robin Hayward. "I hope they come out," he says, referring to the German ships that escaped the previous night, "because we're ready and willing. I hate it when they disappear like that."

In the engine room below, Lieutenant Theodore Izard is thinking about his wife, Pam, now safely settled with his parents in Victoria, British Columbia. The two had met and married in Plymouth six months earlier. Now she's on the other side of the world waiting to start their new life together. "It shouldn't be long before *Athabaskan* goes to Canada," he says hopefully. "Admiral Nelles said it would be soon, and then we'll have a real honeymoon. Boy! What a day that'll be." He touches the picture of his bride and puts it lovingly in his breast pocket.

At 2:00 a.m. on April 29, the Tribals are in position and start patrolling. Radar is unreliable for some unknown reason, and all watches visually rake the waves for any sight or sound of enemy ships. German ships have been reported to be travelling westward at 20 knots between St. Malo and

Roche Douvres. The Canadians are ready for them, both crews anxious for a rematch.

Up on *Haida*'s bridge, De Wolf stands alone with binoculars in his hands. Some distance away, on his right, with head and shoulders silhouetted in the moonlight, is the officer of the watch. The two are silent as their eyes study the coastline. De Wolf looks nervously over at the sister ship, the *Athabaskan*. She is gleaming silver in the moonlight, and the captain knows that if she stands out to him, then she is in full sight of anyone onshore.

At 3:00 a.m. an officer from the bridge on the *Haida* comes aft and stops to have a cup of kye with the surgeon lieutenant in sick bay. "Quiet night so far," he informs the doctor. "We're about 20 metres off Ile de Bas. Should be heading home soon. I'll be glad when we do. I've had a hunch of trouble coming all night. Still, it's not likely anything will happen now," he adds and laughs nervously.

A second signal from Plymouth Headquarters at 3:07 a.m. orders the Tribals to intercept the enemy ships. The crews' senses heighten. New energy is put forth with the news. It's now obvious that they are heading in to finish the battle that was started a few nights ago. All hands are alert and at action stations. Hearts are pumping, and the ship and men become of one mind.

Bunker B, much to his disgust, has been banished to one of the seaman's quarters. They still haven't outfitted him with a life jacket as yet, and Norman Goodale hopes he will be okay.

The enemy ships are now in sight, and at 4:12 a.m., the *Haida* opens fire with starshell lighting up the sky. Two minutes later the *T-24* and *T-27* are sighted racing westward and the chase is on. "There they are!" someone yells. "Load! Load! LOAD!"

The Canadians open up with all guns in a wild chase after the enemy. The Jerries lay a smoke screen and regroup in its shelter while continuing to shoot torpedoes at the Allied ships. All the Allied torpedoes are pointed at the other German Ebling. The crews on the Tribals cheer, yelling that the German torpedo man must be on the side of the Allies.

The Germans hammer at the Canadians with their main guns. The *Athabaskan* seems to be the enemy's target. German starshell bursts over her and salvoes whiz through her rigging, splashing in the water around her. Lieutenant Commander Dunn Lantier, the radar officer, is informed by his radar operator that two objects starboard are heading in their direction and travelling fast. Thirty seconds later, explosions rock the Tribal, and John Laidler, the radar operator, is blown overboard by the force. When he rises to the surface of the water, he's coughing and choking on fuel. It's stinging his eyes and burning his throat. He tries to call out, but realizes that no one can hear him as the *Athabaskan* is 300 metres away and still moving. Even with fuel in his eyes, he can see that her "X" and "Y" guns are destroyed and that her gun crews are wiped out. Smoke is rising from her port side and something about the way she's riding the waves says she is in real trouble. Fortunately, Laidler finds a Kisbie buoy and clings to it. All he can do is wait in the frigid water and hope someone finds him as he watches his ship slow until she lies dead in the water with flames reaching into the night sky.

Meanwhile, unaware of her sister ship's plight, the *Haida* continues the chase, hammering on the fleeing enemy with her guns. From the bridge, Commander De Wolf is planning his next move when he gets word from Lieutenant Commander Stubbs, "We seem to be badly damaged aft."

The message is punctuated by German guns closing in for the kill. The *Haida* crew watch in horror until the torpedo control officer asks the captain, "Why don't we make smoke?"

As the *Haida* swings to starboard, a stoker crawls out on the afterdeck. Braving the blast from the "Y" guns he reaches up and opens the valve, turning on the chemical smoke producers. They work immediately. The *Haida* begins belching white clouds of chemical smoke, then circles the *Athabaskan*, desperately trying to provide cover for the Tribal. The *Haida* steers valiantly between her wounded sister and the enemy while attacking the Germans with enthusiasm. Her crew fires round after round until *T-24*, badly hit, limps to the east. The *T-27* breaks away to the south, with *Haida* on her trail.

During this time, the *Athabaskan* drifts at the mercy of the currents as her men work fiendishly to save her. The fire at the stern ignites the ammunition. Exploding shells and shrapnel fly in all directions. Smoke and flames reach hungrily into the sky, a beacon for the enemy. The *Haida's* smoke screen helps some, but it fails to hide her sister ship completely. The shore batteries open up, and the *Athabaskan* becomes the target of a turkey shoot.

Even in the thick of the ammunition flying overhead, the well-trained men remain calm. With Canadian determination, every man is working to save the ship.

Lieutenant Commander Lantier then fires the last round of starshell from "B" gun. It's the last round ever fired from the broken ship.

There is feverish activity on the crippled ship's decks. Up forward, the bosun's party works frantically to rig the towing hawser. The 70-ton portable pump is pulled into position amidships. The feedline is hoisted overboard and several men make their way aft to fight the raging flames. The wounded are helped below for medical attention. On the bridge, Lieutenant Commander Stubbs is calmly giving orders. The *Athabaskan* is settling deeper into the water and her time is running out. Stubb sighs, then gives the order: "Prepare to abandon ship! All hands stand by their Abandon Ship Stations!"

The men proceed silently to their stations, scarcely able to believe the order they have just heard. A signalman's life jacket strap is loose and an officer bends over the man to snug it up for him. The captain remains on the bridge and watches them go. One of the men has the ship's cat. At the last second he jumps into the waves and is seen swimming toward the French coastline.

Suddenly, a torpedo rips into the hull of the floundering Canadian ship. First Lieutenant Lawrence, on his way to the bridge, is killed instantly. A horrific roar erupts as ammunition, fuel, and tanks explode, creating a huge blowtorch aimed skyward. It is nothing short of a holocaust. The deck tilts and then collapses as internal explosions blow it outwards with heat that melts the metal.

When it's over only one man on deck is still alive. A 19-year-old stoker, Ernest Takalo, is lying on the deck facing the bridge section. The flash burn lights up the entire deck. It is so bright, in fact, that Takalo can see the individual hair strokes from the paint job on the steel plating of the forecastle. Lieutenant William Clark, climbing down from the bridge to the signal deck, is hit with a ball of flame that scoops him overboard. Observers on the *Haida*, which is still pursuing the enemy, see a bright flash. They hear an incredible explosion, and with one voice they gasp at the funnel of flames and smoke. "My God," they cry, "It's the *Athabaskan*!"

The *Haida* shudders in the shock wave, and an escaped Bunker B, terrified by the noise and fear around him, leaps off the deck and into the waves, never to be seen again.

From No. 1 boiler back, the *Athabaskan* is a blazing inferno. What went up with the force of the explosion is now raining burning blobs of fuel on the survivors of the crippled ship. Men run, blindly screaming and beating at the flames landing on them from above. In desperation, many leap headfirst into the sea. The smell of burning of flesh is mixed with the stench of burning oil. And the sound of the crackling flames licking at the vessel is amplified by the sizzle of burning bodies meeting the cold ocean waves.

The ship lurches violently and most of those who are still on board tumble helplessly over the side. "Abandon ship! All hands abandon ship!" the captain yells hoarsely. The gunner's mate hears the order while he is leaning against a railing. He tries to vault over it into the water below, but his arm is broken in two places and won't support his weight. With blood streaming from a gash on his head he looks dumbly at the rail, trying to understand why he can't leap overboard. The ship heels over and he sits down heavily. Feeling queasy and slightly detached from the reality of the situation, he lies down and gravity slides him under the rail and into the sea.

Nineteen-year-old Seaman James Aikins is in the carpenter's shop when he hears the order. He can't escape, as the deck door is jammed tight. Running through the mess to the passageway, he reaches out to open the No. 2 boiler room door and it explodes in his hand. He is thrown backwards and drenched by a scalding spray of water, sustaining burns to most of his body. He slides down the guardrail and drops his scalded body into the frigid waters below. Fighting for consciousness, he manages to grab onto some debris. He clings to it for dear life.

"Abandon ship! Abandon ship!" That heart-stopping cry in the night — the blast of explosions, the sizzle of flesh, and the smell of death — signals the end of the mighty and proud *Athabaskan.*

But what of her men?

# Chapter 9
# Abandoned Ship, Abandoned Survivors

Stoker Robert Gracie and his shipmates waste no time in obeying the order to abandon ship. The HMCS *Athabaskan* is sinking. The shock is traumatic as the group hits the water, but the bold survivors swim valiantly away from the doomed ship. Stoker Gracie is swimming frantically. He can hear the main mast creaking and ripping, and he knows it's falling. Looking up, he sees it looming above him and with renewed strength he strikes out at the water. There's a mighty splash and a whoosh of water overtakes him, but the mast itself falls clear.

Almost completely engulfed in flames, the *Athabaskan* lists horribly and sinks deeper into the water. Chief Petty Officer William Mitchell is still aboard, pinned to the main deck by a heavy beam. Both legs are crushed, the pain is almost more than he can bear. He calls out but in the noise and confusion no one seems to notice him. Suddenly, Able Seaman Donald Newman and Leading Signalman Allen Thrasher appear out of the smoke like angels. They work feverishly, using a steel bar for leverage, and soon Mitchell is free and sliding over the side and into the water. Newman yells down at him apologetically as Mitchell hits the water. "That's all we can do for you," he says, then disappears back into the smoke. Using only his arms, with his legs drifting uselessly behind him, Mitchell pulls himself through the freezing ocean waves to a safe distance. Without a doubt, he knows that if he makes it, he'll owe his life to those two mates.

A group of men are frantically trying to activate the *Athabaskan's* motor launch when the pulleys jam. Able Seaman Russell Phillips crawls underneath to yank the launch loose. Pulling with all his might, he doesn't realize that there is nothing supporting the heavy boat. Suddenly it comes crashing down on him, breaking his arm and dislocating his shoulder. The others rally around and soon the boat is launched. Phillips is lowered gently over the side into the water.

In the forecastle of the *Athabaskan*, gobs of flaming fuel are raining down on Able Seamen Samuel Fillatre and Lester McKeeman, but they refuse to leave the area until they first get their gun captain, Leading Seaman "Buck" Parsons, safely over the side. Meanwhile, Able Seaman Laidler, continuing to hold tightly to his Kisbie buoy, watches the *Athabaskan* through her final ordeal. He hears the sounds of her destruction, as ruptured watertight bulkheads cave in under the deadly weight of water, and machinery tears away from normally secure bedplates. The *Athabaskan*, in her final death throes, cries like a child. And it feels to Laidler like he is watching a friend dying in agony. The ship had guarded and protected him from the very beginning. Now he is helpless to save her. Choked with emotion and grief, Laidler turns his face against the buoy and closes his eyes.

As the Tribal tilts slowly to a vertical position, gear and equipment begin to crash like stones and boulders cascading down the side of a mountain. Each and every item — pots, pans, and tools — clatters and bangs as it slides and tumbles. The great ship moans. And suddenly, above the cacophony, comes a loud and very distinctive crash. "There goes the piano!" shouts a voice in the darkness.

Now vertical, the ship seems to poise there a moment and then slips swiftly backwards, down into the encompassing waters with a sizzling hiss. The Tribal Class Destroyer disappears and darkness envelopes the sea and its survivors. Their ship, their home, their friend, is dead, sunk beneath the ocean she once ruled, to rest in its depths in a cold and watery grave. Only those trapped in her final moments keep her company.

While the *Athabaskan* endures her agony, the *Haida* loses no time in hunting down the enemy ships, which had fled in different directions. Harassed by the Canadian Tribal's fire, the *T-24* speeds eastward while the *T-27* makes off to the south. The *Haida* fires a direct hit and continues to fire unmercifully on the *T-27*. If her gunners had been fast before, they are fighting desperately now. "For the *Athabaskan!*" they yell as they load and fire.

"Another hit!" Flames leap high on the first German destroyer and it smoulders in the smoke. The second enemy ship slows and falls behind the first. Suddenly, in the heat of battle, the *Haida* is illuminated by a strange bright light, which is followed by a rumbling noise astern. Her frantic men above deck pause momentarily to look. It's too bright for starshell and their gaze is greeted by a deadly rising column of white smoke. Higher and higher it bursts from the sea, flames, smoke, and debris shooting into the air. "My God!" the crew of the *Haida* gasps. "There goes the *Athabaskan!*"

Able Seaman David Gold is stunned by the horrific sight, and he gazes in shock and disbelief, wondering at the holocaust that has destroyed his ship's sister. "We're next for sure," he groans to his shipmates. They turn and fight in earnest now, desperate to get the upper hand of the battle so they can begin to search for survivors.

The *Haida* is closing the gap between her and the German ship. The *T-27* is beginning to show the effects of the devastating shelling. Flames are leaping from her hull as the fleeing enemy comes dangerously close to the French coast-line. Suddenly, without warning, she swings around toward the *Haida* in a bold attempt to escape the trap. But then *T-27* slows and stops completely, leaning to port at an even sharper angle than before. The grim rocky shores of Finistrere have caught her. She's run aground.

Realizing that further action is pointless and that the other German ship has escaped, Commander De Wolf orders a ceasefire and heads back to where the *Athabaskan* was last seen.

Disregarding the threat of enemy ships, De Wolf orders his illumination officer to fire one starshell for a better look at the situation. It reveals nothing. The *Athabaskan* is nowhere to be seen. As the flare dies out, scores of life jacket lights dot the waves. The mighty *Athabaskan* is nowhere to be seen. All that is left is a spattering of survivors fighting to stay alive, broken and freezing in the unforgiving Atlantic.

The crew of the *Haida*, stricken with grief, rushes to save the survivors.

The *Haida* eases gently into the mass of struggling seamen and stops. "We'll stop for 15 minutes, under orders from Plymouth," states the commander. Headquarters has ordered the *Haida* to leave by daybreak.

The sight imbeds itself on the rescuers. Men — friends — grouped in the waves below are yelling, blowing whistles, and shouting for the *Haida* to help them. For those on the ship's sides, it's possible to climb aboard using the scramble nets, but for those in front or in the rear, it's a different story. A light wind is causing the *Haida* to drift away faster than the men can swim to her, and rescue seems cruelly out of reach. The seriously wounded are helpless, at the mercy of others. Even the uninjured are having trouble making it to safety. The friendly ship's propellers are put in motion to manoeuvre closer and correct the drift, but they're shut down quickly and survivors are being sucked in by the mighty slicing of the screws.

Those not ordered to man the guns or keep watch above are forming lines to pull the men from the water. The deck is now smeared with oil, and everyone who has contact with the survivors is soon covered in it as well. The fumes are unbelievable, and injuries, burns, and cuts are instantly covered in the stinking, stinging, and sometimes smouldering fuel.

Leading Cook Bernard Laurin had thrown himself off the deck of the *Athabaskan* right before she sank. He had come up choking and gagging from the oil and salt water he had swallowed. Laurin swims as far from the wreck as possible. He rubs his eyes, trying to free them of fuel. He thinks briefly of his family and wonders how they will feel to hear that he went down with his ship. Then, with renewed vigour, he strikes out for a float. With burned and swollen fingers he grasps onto the side. If anyone survives, it will be him. He is determined not put his wife and family through the heartache if he can help it.

A few moments later, Lieutenant Commander Stubbs swims up to him. He says that he has been blown off the bridge. Laurin notices the captain's face and hands are burned, but otherwise Stubbs appears to be in reasonable condition. Then, out of the darkness, the *Haida* comes into view. "Swim for it, son," the captain orders, and Laurin swims until he is scooped up into friendly arms and ushered below deck to warm blankets and tots of rum.

Lieutenant William Clark and Sub-Lieutenant Robert Annett strike out from their Carley float when the *Haida* appears. Soon the exhausted men realize they can't make it to the ship. Grasping a cork net, Clark looks around for his companion and sees only water. Annett is nowhere to be seen. Clark realizes he is now among 14 other men. By dawn only four are left. In the pale light, Clark sees a nearby Carley float, swims over to it, and paddles back to pull the remaining three survivors off the cork net and into the raft, away from hypothermia and death.

Petty Officer George Casswell drifts away from the main group after a few hours in the water. Alone and giving up hope, he is unaware of the *Haida* and the rescue going on a short distance away. As his body temperature lowers, he experiences a feeling of warmth and well-being. Beyond exhausted, he starts thinking how nice it would be simply to let go and drift off to sleep. Thinking of his family gathering together for his memorial, he shocks himself awake. To fight off death, he starts reciting the Lord's Prayer over and over again.

Suddenly the *Haida*'s cutter appears and the half-frozen sailor is hauled aboard. "Canadian or German?" Casswell demands. "Cause if you're damn Nazis, then toss me back in the water."

"I assure you, we're Canadians. The *Haida* is right over there waiting for us to bring you in." Casswell smiles, then promptly collapses.

The men on the *Haida* who are ordered to stand by their battle positions, such as Petty Officer Fred Polischuk, watch the rescue going on below them with feelings of helplessness. Their friends and fellow Canadians need them. Yet, with daybreak kissing the night sky, they have to stay where they are in case of trouble. With every tick of the clock, the danger to all of them grows. Every last life raft, life jacket, and life boat, have been tossed overboard for the survivors. If attacked, the crew of the *Haida* will have to pray. Every single man left on board is well aware that there will be no surviving a sinking ship without that emergency equipment.

Hearing the men's desperate pleas, the rescuers increase their efforts. The minutes are ticking by, but there are so many men in the water. It's obvious to everyone that not all of them will be pulled aboard in time. The minutes slip by far too quickly and they work diligently against the threat of daylight. A rescue line of strong young hands and arms reaches out to grasp the oil-soaked survivors.

Lieutenant Commander Stubbs moves in amongst his men in the water. All he can do is offer them words of encouragement and inspire them to keep struggling against death. Swimming close to the nets on the lee side of the *Haida*, he looks up at the sky. Dawn is breaking. The ship is now vulnerable to shore batteries and German destroyers. He is filled with panic. "Get out of here, *Haida*! E-boats!" Again, he yells desperately to the *Haida*. "Do you hear me? Get the hell out of here!"

It is the last command he will ever give. John Hamilton Stubbs, the commander of the fated *Assiniboine*, and the last commander of the mighty *Athabaskan*, swims off into the awakening dawn and is never seen alive again.

Rough and ready sailors, with salty language and sea-hardened hands, gently cut clothing off the wounded, and tenderly wash fuel out of eyes and injuries. They spoon-feed hot liquids into the chilled, and rub down cold bodies, bringing back heat and feeling, and then cover them with blankets. More than one wipes away tears as friends who succumbed to the elements are brought on board, lifeless and still.

The 15 minutes comes and goes. De Wolf paces on the bridge, watching the horizon with nervous and anxious eyes. There isn't going to be enough time. With more sailors brought on board, and less emergency equipment available, one torpedo could bring catastrophe to all those they have rescued. Not to mention jeopardizing the life of his ship and his men. Bobbing lights, spread far and wide, show too many men still in the water. Men who might never make it. Shouting down encouragement, he glances for enemy ships, urging on the rescuers, yelling for the men to move faster ... swim harder ... haul up the injured quicker.

The first streaks of dawn are finally breaking through. Sunrise is moments away, and with every ticking minute, the *Haida* and the rescue operation become sitting ducks. Still, the captain orders five more minutes — five more precious minutes.

"I'll warn you every minute," he adds to the order. His compassion has won the moment, but common sense dictates that time has come to an end. The crew gets a short reprieve to collect as many survivors as possible. Then Plymouth and fate will have to decide what the next move will be.

Able Seaman Digby Deal is hauled aboard, oily and cold, but uninjured. He helps get Lieutenant Jack Scott safely on deck. But when the men start cutting away Scott's clothing, Digby bolts for the ocean. "Are you kidding?" yells the seaman as Digby scrambles down the net.

"My friend Moar is still out there and I can't leave him behind. I promised him." He jumps back into the waves and swims to a Carley float. Able Seaman Raymond Moar has a broken back. Without assistance he will never make it.

At the same time De Wolf calls out the minutes.

"Just one more moment," thinks Commander De Wolf to himself. But the *Haida*'s asdic operator notifies him of the possibility of approaching enemy craft. Commander De Wolf has no choice. "Slow ahead," he orders, staring straight ahead.

Men still in the water panic as the *Haida* starts up the engines. They are begging, pleading, yelling curses. Fighting for their lives, they swim to reach the nets and ropes still hanging off the side of the destroyer. Commander De Wolf has already disregarded three orders to leave the area. He now has absolutely no choice. He prays silently for those he leaves behind, knowing their cries from the still-darkened sea will haunt his nights forever.

The *Haida* trembles and vibrates as the turbines throb. Petty Officer H.P. Murray and Telegraphist S.A. Turner are still on one of the scramble nets trying to rescue the survivors as the ship starts to move. They look at the hands reaching out to them and grab for just one more. The ocean current around their legs gets stronger and, handing off the last of the survivors, they both struggle to unhook themselves from the nets. The waves are now waist high, and the force is making it impossible to climb up. Hands from above reach down, gripping ... pulling ... tugging ... but it's no use. The *Haida* picks up speed and suddenly the rope breaks. The wake surges over the two men and washes them straight into the turning screws.

The handful of men on deck look after them in stunned silence. It is too much to comprehend that these two lads, who have played such a courageous part in saving so many of the survivors from the *Athabaskan*, should meet this terrible fate after such heroism.

Able Seaman George Howard is swimming close to the *Haida* when she begins to move. The wake of the destroyer threatens to drown him. As the *Haida* pulls away, 22-year-old Able Seaman Ted Hewitt is frantically trying to shed his heavier clothing. He struggles for every breath, taking in gulps of sea water mixed with fuel. He gasps and chokes, arms caught in the sleeves of his greatcoat, the frigid Atlantic tugging him down to where his beloved ship lies. Despair engulfs him and looking around he sees over 100 pairs of eyes all watching the departing ship with the same hopelessness that he is feeling.

Hewitt is sure that if the *Haida* leaves without him, his life is over. With all his might he swims for a loose line and hangs on, yelling with all his strength. Someone on deck notices his body being slammed against the wake and calls his crew mates to help haul the man up the side. The Atlantic has other ideas. Time after time the waves seem to reach out and grab the man, threatening to snatch him back to the waters below. Still, he hangs on. Finally, they have him aboard. He is the last survivor of the *Athabaskan* to be rescued by the *Haida*.

Meanwhile, right after the cutter has been dropped by the departing ship for the survivors to climb into, Acting Leading Seaman William McClure, Able Seaman Jack Hannan, and Stoker William Cummings decide to jump in and help with the rescue efforts. McClure assumes command of the cutter and orders a slow ahead to look for survivors. Petty Officer Casswell is the first to be picked up, followed by Able Seamen Jean Audet, Stanley Buck, and Charles Burgess, as well as Signalmen Thomas Eady and Guy Norris.

Shortly after, the cutter's engine sputters, backfires, and dies. Alone in enemy waters without a ship in sight, the men hit, kick, curse, and play with the motor to get it to start again. But the motor stubbornly refuses to fire. As the cutter drifts, more survivors are found and pulled aboard. Murray and Turner, who were washed off the net when the *Haida* pulled away, had managed to avoid the churning screws and had drifted out on the swells. They are only in the water five minutes when the cutter finds them.

By now, the *Haida* has set course for Plymouth, leaving the grave of her sister ship far behind. Below decks, in the dim light of the battle lamps, is an unforgettable sight. Survivors are everywhere in the confined quarters. In the after flats the air reeks with the stench of fuel oil. No heat can be turned on and no smoking is permitted below decks for fear of fire.

The *Haida* had rescued 42 of the *Athabaskan*'s crewmembers. So, for the doctor and his assistants, the work is only beginning. Morphine is administered to the men with the worst injuries, and cleaning the fuel-fed wounds is a challenge. The badly injured and those who were crushed by the ship in its last minutes of life can only be made comfortable until they reach harbour. One man, badly injured, is taken to the captain's cabin for a blood transfusion because he is not going to survive to see a hospital without one. All on board know that over 200 of their friends and shipmates are still lying in or below the waves.

Able Seaman Wilfred Henrickson still clings to the side of a Carley float, but wonders why he is bothering. His head is drooping into the sea and he's swallowing oil and water. Exhausted, he is ready to die. There is no room on the float and no rescue in sight. On the float, Able Seaman William Bint sees the hopelessness in the young man's face and convinces him to trade places for a bit.

The Carley floats and cork net floats gradually become less and less crowded as men give up, or give out. These men slide silently beneath the waves. Floating corpses bump lightly against the living, adding a touch of the macabre to the scene. The living are floating face up. The dead face down. Those who are dead are reverently pushed aside to make room for the living. Mourning will come later — if there is a later.

Far away from the main groups, two lonely figures bob on the swells. Thirty-four-year-old Able Seaman Lester McKeeman (an old man in the eyes of his shipmates, who call him "Pappy") is supporting a young injured sailor on his back, trying to keep the boy's spirits up by talking to him. They babble about home, families, friends, shipmates, and a host of other things. Occasionally there is silence as the teenaged *Athabaskan* crew member lapses into unconsciousness. His laboured breathing is now the only sign of life in him. McKeeman is trying to hang on for the kid's sake. If he were alone, he thinks, he would no longer be alive. The waves lapping and pulling at him are slowly winning. Right now, death is almost welcome. He is so very tired.

When daylight breaks and the first rays of sunlight creep across the water, McKeeman's young friend has grown still. Sobbing for himself as much as for the lad, McKeeman unhooks the death-stiffened fingers from around his neck and lets the lifeless form drift silently away. "Christ Jesus Almighty — forgive me!" sobs the seaman. It's one of the most agonizing things he has ever had to do. And, with the dying of the young one, he feels a part of himself die too.

Finally, German ships are seen approaching. Their rescuers have come in the form of their enemies. For all those survivors left behind by the Allied forces, the POW camps await them. One of the ships that comes to their rescue is the *T-24*.

Far out in the Channel, the *Haida*'s cutter is slowly making its way home. The men are wet and cold. But with hard tack, water, and malted milk tablets, they are better off than those left at the site of the sinking. Suddenly, on the horizon looms a German mine sweeper that changes course and heads directly for the small boat. Darting into a mine field, the men pray the Germans will give up. For a moment it looks as though the vessel is planning to fire on them. It hesitates, then swings around. leaving the survivors to their fate. Every man on that little boat knows their situation is desperate and that the odds are against them.

The *Haida*'s cutter is finally sighted by a squadron of RAF planes and the exhausted survivors are picked up by an Air/ Sea Rescue launch and taken to Penzance. By midnight they are resting, warm, and comfortable. But a disquieting thought stays with them all, "What about the rest of the gang?"

That question, for some, comes many years after the war. Commander Stubbs's body washed ashore with 59 others near Plouescat, Brittany, and they were all buried nearby. Under the cover of night, 1000 people from all over the French island gathered together to mark the seamen's graves with a cascade of beautiful flowers — a gesture of their respect for *les libérateurs canadiens.*

# Epilogue

Able-Bodied Seaman Norman Goodale, who served on the *Haida* in 1944, has since relived those two nights, over and over again. To this day, he can still hear the cries of the men in the water, calling out from the waves. Goodale married and came back to Canada after the war, and 20 years later he settled in a subdivision in a small town in Quebec. Soon after moving in, he found out that a few doors down lived Dan Wiggins, a gunners mate and survivor from the *Athabaskan*. Subsequently, the two families spent many hours together, and the two men spoke frequently of that fateful night the *Athabaskan* was lost.

Around this same time, Norm and his wife, Joan, decided they needed some work done on their house. They called a man one street over who was a carpenter. A German by the name of Willy Zerter came over and saw the picture of Norm in his World War II navy uniform. It didn't take the three men long to discover that Willy had been a gunner on the *T-27*, the German destroyer that had been beached at Mencham off Kerlouan by the *Haida* during the night the *Athabaskan* went down.

"My Commander, Kapitanleutnant Gotzmann commented on how quickly and accurately the British shot that night," Willy told his new Canadian friends. "We beached on

124

purpose to avoid the firing. We had no idea the ships were Canadian, only that they were bull dogs."

"We were the Royal Canadian Navy," Norm said quietly, "a force to be proud of, a force to be reckoned with."

# Further Reading

Burrow, Len. *Unlucky Lady.* Canada's Wings, Inc., 1982.

Douglas, W.A.B. and Brereton Greenhous. *Out of the Shadows.* Dundurn Press, 1996.

Ireland, Bernard. *Naval History of WWII.* HarperCollins Publishers, 1998.

Lamb, James B. *The Corvette Navy.* Toronto: The Macmillan Company of Canada, 1988.

Lawrence, Hal. *A Bloody War.* Toronto: The Macmillan Company of Canada Limited, 1979.

Lord, Walter. *The Miracle of Dunkirk.* Penguin Books, 1982.

Nelson, CPO Mark. *The History of the Naval Reserve in Winnipeg 1923–2003: Winnipeg's Navy.*

Richards, Lieut. Commander (Mad) S.T.R. *Operation Sick Bay.* Cantaur Publishing, 1994.

# Acknowledgments

I would like to thank W.A. Fogg for the photos in this book and his interview regarding his time spent on the HMCS *Minas* and *Waskesiu*. I would also like to thank Norm Goodale, John Jeffrey Coates from the HMCS *Haida*, John Lipton, and a number of Navy veterans who wish to be nameless. They shared their stories and their history with me, an experience I will always treasure.

# Photo Credits

# About the Author

Cynthia J. Faryon lives in Richer, Manitoba with her husband, youngest daughter, and their two dogs.

# Amazing Author Question and Answer

## What was your inspiration for writing about the heroes of the Royal Canadian Navy?

My father was in the Air Force during WWII. I grew up hearing him yelling in the night from nightmares on occasion, especially after watching a war movie. We weren't permitted to chew gum, crunch potato chips, or set off fireworks because his nerves were so bad. We all knew it was because of shell shock during the war, but my father would never talk about his experiences. After he passed away in 1988, I started digging into his past and discovered his amazing story. I only wished I could have learned about it from him while he was alive, and by writing these books, I'm hoping to help others discover their own family heroes while they are still alive.

## What surprised you most while you were conducting your research?

How interesting Canadian history is when you personalize it. WWII was always nothing more than boring statistics to me as a child growing up. Putting faces to the men who fought the famous battles and discovering the human side of the war makes it so real.

## What do you most admire about the people in this Amazing Story?

They are simply ordinary people who rose to greatness under duress. To go into a veteran's home and see him as a nice, elderly gentleman, a grandfatherly type, then to hear his story of battle and survival is incredible. People have so many sides to them I find it fascinating.

## Did you run into any difficulties while researching this book?

Finding veterans still alive and willing to talk about their experiences was a challenge. The Internet became my best tool. I sent out emails to various organizations and posted messages on many, many sites. It gave me access to veterans all over. Through emails and phone calls I was able to reach many men in this book. Every time I found one of them and spoke to them on the phone I felt humbled, excited, and honoured. I felt I already knew them.

## What part of the writing process did you enjoy most?

Weaving the human story from the facts, dates, and technical history. Putting the real person with his feelings, fears, and deeds into the story so the reader will feel like he or she has gotten to know him personally.

## Why did you become a writer? Who inspired you?

My mother and my father's rich past. My mother was an orphan and separated from her sister for 65 years. The two were reunited by accident, and after meeting my aunt for the first time and hearing her life story, I knew I had to write a book about it. So I wrote Sisters Torn, and when that was finished I felt something was missing from my life. So I started to freelance, and then started writing for Amazing Stories.

## What is your next project?

Another Amazing Story, titled *Unsung Heroes of the Canadian Army*. And after that I have some ideas for fiction.

## Who are your Canadian heroes?

The real Canadian heroes are those who touch us emotionally with their lives and their integrity. Among the Canadians who have influenced me the most are Terry Fox, Rick Hanson, and my father, Lawrence Cramer.

## Which other Amazing Stories titles would you recommend?

All of them. This is a great series and should be in every household and every school. We have a rich history and Canadians need to become more aware of our amazing country and those who have made it what it is.

AMAZING STORIES™

# UNSUNG HEROES OF THE ROYAL CANADIAN AIR FORCE

Incredible Tales of Courage and
Daring During World War II

HISTORY
by Cynthia J. Faryon

# UNSUNG HEROES OF THE ROYAL CANADIAN AIR FORCE
## Incredible Tales of Courage and Daring During World War II

*"That he was a hero is merely incidental to the fact that he died in pain — that he was robbed of life — and that he is lost to his generation. There is glory in living for an ideal as well as in dying for it."* Hector Bolitho, 1946

More than 250,000 courageous men and women were enlisted in the Royal Canadian Air Force during World War II. These Canadians fought valiantly in every major air operation from the Battle of Britain to the bombing of Germany. Thousands lost their lives. Those who survived to tell their stories were forever changed. Here are some of their incredible stories.

True stories. Truly Canadian.

ISBN 1-55153-977-2

AMAZING STORIES™

# CANADIAN SPIES

Tales of Espionage in Nazi-Occupied
Europe During World War II

HISTORY

by Tom Douglas

# CANADIAN SPIES
## Tales of Espionage in Nazi-Occupied Europe During World War II

*"Dumais sprang to his feet and began running away from the direction of the train. This time, he was spotted and bullets screamed by his head. When he reached a dense clump of bushes, he dived into them and held his breath."*

During World War II, some of the most treacherous jobs were those performed by men and women located deep within enemy territory. Always in danger of being exposed and subjected to torture, imprisonment, and even death, their stories are chilling accounts of bravery and luck — and, in some cases, what happens when the luck runs out.

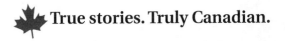 True stories. Truly Canadian.

ISBN 1-55153-966-7

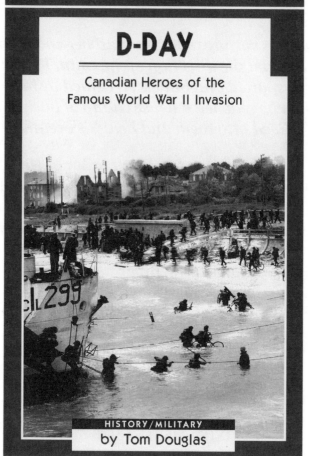

AMAZING STORIES™

# D-DAY

### Canadian Heroes of the
### Famous World War II Invasion

HISTORY/MILITARY
by Tom Douglas

# D-DAY
## Canadian Heroes of the
## Famous World War II Invasion

*"As the Canadian armour neared the highway,
Meyer yelled 'Attack!' and all hell broke loose."*

On June 6, 1944, a daring and ambitious invasion
of Europe changed the course of World War II,
eventually leading to the surrender of Nazi Germany. During the night, through storms and high
seas, the Allied forces swept towards the beaches
of Normandy in France. This is the story of the
bravery, the heroism, and the sheer dumb luck
of the more than 14,000 Canadians who played a
crucial role in that incredible event.

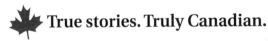 True stories. Truly Canadian.

ISBN 1-55153-795-8

# KLONDIKE JOE BOYLE
## Heroic Adventures From
## Gold Fields to Battlefields

*"...man with the heart of a Viking
and the simple faith of a child."*
Joe Boyle epitaph

An adventurer and a natural leader, Joe White-side Boyle blazed the White Pass to the Yukon and was among the few who scratched a fortune from the Klondike. During World War I, he was a spymaster working behind Russian lines. He cheated death many times to become the "Saviour of Rumania," and in the process fell in love with a queen.

 True stories. Truly Canadian.

ISBN 1-55153-969-1

# OTHER AMAZING STORIES

These titles are available wherever you buy books. If you have trouble finding the book you want, call the Altitude order desk at **1-800-957-6888**, e-mail your request to: **orderdesk@altitudepublishing.com** or visit our Web site **at www.amazingstories.ca**

New AMAZING STORIES titles are published every month.

# GREAT MILITARY LEADERS
## Charismatic Canadian Commanders

*"I never saw his equal for true grit…He lay all day with his body torn and bleeding, and it was only at night when the stretcher bearers could approach the trench to get out the wounded that he was carried away, and then he went last."*

The history of Canada is filled with charismatic and talented military leaders. Each of the men featured in this collection was wildly successful in business and used his private wealth to provide Canada with a military unit at its times of greatest need. Today these respected units continue to serve Canada and Canadians.

 True stories. Truly Canadian.

ISBN 1-55153-773-7

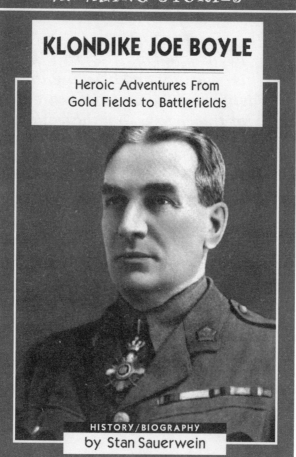